DEDICATION

By Craig Nehring

Early in 2014 I was chatting on a dating site with a woman named Rene Pawelko from Rhinelander, Wisconsin. We talked for about three weeks before we decided to meet each other.

When I arrived at her front door, I thought that she was the most beautiful woman I had seen in a long time. I opened the car door and she got in. She was going to hang out with me for the weekend.

On the way back to my place in New London we had time to talk and get to know each other. She explained that before I took interest in her, she wanted me to be aware of the fact that she had a tumor on her spinal cord. She had been diagnosed with cancer in 2005 at the young age of 24. Although it was smaller in size now, she believed that she could die before some of the rest of us. I was all right with that; not getting to know her would be much worse.

We would spend weeks together, and later she would stay with me in New London. We went fishing at my dad's place in Woodruff, Wisconsin where she had so much fun catching panfish. We went to movies and cooked together. It was not long after we met that we fell in love.

Rene also loved to go on ghost investigations with us. I was surprised when she wanted to ride along to

Mansfield Prison in Ohio with the Fox Valley Ghost Hunters (FVGH) team as it was a long drive and her pain medications made her very tired.

Mansfield is where *The Shawshank Redemption* was filmed. Rene had so much fun taking pictures of the place as well as the new-born geese that had just hatched on the property. She also collected pretty stones and saved them in a bag to take home at the end of the trip. Rene touched all my team members with her kind heart and very caring ways.

Rene and I had a special bond; we loved each other through good times and bad. We talked on the phone every night telling stories of the day, and always said we loved each other. I picked the name "Pookie" for her. She said she didn't want to be referred to as Garfield's stuffed animal, so I picked another name, "Munchkin." She loved it. On my birthday and at Christmas she would make gifts for me from her heart, signed "From your little Munchkin." I will cherish them forever.

Rene was a very caring person; even though she was sick. She would care for me when I didn't feel well. Once I was so sick that I couldn't eat. She told me to lie down, and she would make me some soup. Though she was really tired and in a lot of pain, she still made sure that I was all right.

I wish I would have known her longer; but even though she was taken so soon, I know she is there watching over me. I talk to her every morning and night because I believe she hears what I say and knows how much I miss her.

Rene enjoyed so many things in life. She loved to create art, and even got to paint with Bob Ross. She loved songs by Taylor Swift as well as our song that we picked together, "All Of Me" by John Legend. Her favorite movies were *My Sisters Keeper* and *If I Stay*. She loved her cats and even trained one to fetch a bottle cap and bring it back to her. I dedicated a song to her as it reflects everything I feel. It's by Faith Hill called "There You'll Be."

Even though she is gone, I feel her in the breeze that blows on my skin and in the changing color of the leaves. I had a chance to talk to Rene three days before she passed away. We were making plans for the weekend. She said that she missed me and loved me very much. In closing she said that she would always be there for me and was always only a phone call away.

I end with this: Rene, my munchkin, wherever you may be I miss you with all my heart. I will always love, and never forget you as long as I live.

Rene Pawelko
June 11, 1981 to Sept 13, 2015

Also, To my mom, dad and sister for always believing in me--gone, but not forgotten.

INTRODUCTION

By Enid Cleaves

It has been said that Wisconsin is one of the leading states in ghost or paranormal activity. From stories told by early Native Americans and European settlers to current happenings and hauntings, almost everyone has had, or knows someone who has had, a paranormal experience. There probably are stories from every county or town in the state. This book covers some of the most notable, the most popular, the most consistent and sometimes unbelievable encounters.

The Fox Valley Ghost Hunters, based in the Appleton area and headed by Craig Nehring, is a non-profit organization that investigates reports of paranormal activities throughout the Midwest. They do not charge for what they do, although they will gladly accept donations to help cover their expenses. Often, after they compile the results from an investigation, FVGH will come back to a business to do a "reveal." This can be a fund raiser for the business as well as a future advertising source. After all, who doesn't want to visit a restaurant, a winery, school, or an old lighthouse that is reported to be haunted?

Allegedly, ghosts have a reason for remaining in buildings or areas they once frequented. It may be fear of moving on: that their existence will end, they might be judged for their misdeeds, or even go to hell. It may be guilt: they died suddenly or unexpectedly, leaving loved ones to grieve. Ghosts may have unfinished business: ensuring that their family is healthy and financially sound. It may be because of an injustice: perhaps the spirit was murdered and wants to stay around for the apprehension and conviction of his/her perpetrator. The explanations are many and varied; but for some reason, ghosts are not ready to leave their old haunts!

Some of you will scoff and say, "I don't believe in those stories; it's all in one's imagination." Some scientists and researchers might agree.

You have probably heard of the Ouija board. Two players sit across from one another with the board on their laps and their finger tips resting lightly on a pointer. A question is asked of the board; the pointer will float over the board and pick a number(s) or letter(s) to spell out an answer. A scientific rebuttal to that credits the ideomotor effect, whereby the power of suggestion causes our muscles to move unconsciously (our fingers might be manipulating the pointer without our knowledge).

Certain religions, as well as many individuals, believe that the board can be a portal for demonic possession. Craig outlaws them in the FVGH group "because no one knows how to open and close them." When it was once mentioned that the team obtain a Ouija board, some members talked of quitting the group. Two team members said that they once used the board, and "something won't leave them alone now." So they burned it and buried the ashes in the ground. The next morning they found the board intact under a tree.

Reportedly, humans can *hear* sounds from 20 to 20,000 Hertz. Below 20, we can *feel* vibrations from the sound waves. Examples of these inaudible waves can be produced by storms, wind, weather pattern, and even appliances that we use daily.

British psychologist Dr. Richard Wiseman, author of *Paranormality: Why We See What Isn't There* claims our eyeballs have a resonant frequency of about 20 Hz. Lower than this frequency our eyeballs will vibrate, possibly causing us to *see* images that aren't there. These waves can be felt in our stomachs as well, producing positive or negative feelings similar to those experienced in a spooky house.

Then there are the cold spots, indications that a ghost may be drawing heat from its surroundings in order to manifest itself. A scientific response is that convection causes objects to lose heat (hot air rises, and cool air drops--the same with humid vs. dry air).

Often, photographers will point to round light-colored spots on their photographs as orbs, balls of light that show spirits who have not passed on. Sometimes photos taken with a flash cause these spots to actually glow. But, have we considered dust specks, bugs, or dirty lenses?

And why do paranormal investigations usually take place after dark? Ghosts are often defined as shadowy figures, so wouldn't they be more difficult to see in the dark? FVGH believes that during the day, the sun will take most of the spirit's energy, making it invisible. After dark, the spirit may use the electrical current in a building. Regardless, it is a lot spookier to search a place using only flashlights.

Scientists might say that an investigation of a few hours is not enough time to perform a valid experiment. Why not? And...wouldn't several individual investigations equal or exceed the hours spent on one investigation?

An ion counter is sometimes used by paranormal groups to detect a spirit's presence based on the belief that ghosts may use ionic energy to materialize. A scientist might say that ions are caused by natural, rather than supernatural, phenomena that can affect our moods and our bodies. Many symptoms reported by people who claim to have paranormal experiences might be caused by high electromagnetic field (emf) radiation that can interact with the ion field, thus affecting each other.

This may be a stretch, but carbon monoxide poisoning can lead to confusion and hallucinations due to oxygen deprivation. To tell the truth, I have never interviewed a person who told of experiencing paranormal experiences while suffering from carbon monoxide poisoning!

The following stories are results of investigations at various Wisconsin locations conducted by the Fox Valley Ghost Hunters, and stories and interviews by Enid Cleaves, "ghost writer" author who has visited many of these same locations and talked with people who have stories of their own encounters with the spiritual world.

Immediately following this introduction, you will find short biographies of Craig Nehring, his present team, and Enid Cleaves.

Brief descriptions of the equipment that the FVGH investigators use in their search for signs of paranormal activities are included at the end of the book. More information can be found about each device on various web sites.

In the following stories some names and places have been changed to respect individual requests to remain anonymous. For example, one story includes information about a FVGH team member who was possessed during an investigation. After she was brought back to her earthly state of mind, she asked that the incident be kept confidential. That team member is no longer with the ghost hunters, yet we continue to protect her anonymity.

Many of these stories take a walk on the dark side so to speak. They are the most supernatural, surreal, sensational and scary. They deal with violence, abuse, and even possession. Often these are reasons that an individual or an owner of a haunted building will invite paranormal teams to investigate.

There are good ghosts too—the benevolent as opposed to the malevolent. An example might be spirits who hang around after their death, maybe to say a lingering goodbye to their loved ones. After my husband died, it was in the form of the small cloud that came out of nowhere and dissipated in front of me as I stood on the upper balcony of my house. With Craig, it was his soul mate who died too young, but communicates with him now on a different plane of existence.

FVGH believes that a *ghost* is someone that is still here on this earth while a *spirit is* one who has crossed over. Dictionaries often use those terms, and others such as apparition, phantom, specter, and soul as one and the same. We use the above-mentioned terms interchangeably in this book.

The cover of this book is done in black and white. Yet, there is no black and white when it comes to subjects dealt with in this book, but rather various shades of gray. We do not try to, or want to, alter your belief system in any way. Regardless, we expect that you will find these stories fascinating and thought-provoking.

The Fox Valley Ghost Hunters would like to thank the following paranormal societies for their collaboration and cooperation in various investigations:

Northern Wisconsin Paranormal Society(NWPS)
Rhinelander, WI

Discovering The Unknown (DTU)
Waukesha, WI

St Croix Paranormal
Stillwater, MN

Dark Sky Paranormal Research
Palatine, IL

Wisconsin/Illinois Paranormal Solutions (W.I.P.S.)
aka Relatively Haunted
Wisconsin Rapids, WI

Fox Valley Ghost Hunters 2
Green Bay, WI

TABLE OF CONTENTS

What Hides in the Berlin Tannery	1
Summerwind Blows Specters In	12
Crib in the Attic	22
Ghosts Vacation at Greenville Station	28
Phantoms Frolic on Franklin Street	34
Anything Goes at Old St. Joe's	43
Inside the Walls of the First Ward School	49
Ghosts Stiehl Stalk the Winery	60
The Secrets of Stevenson Creek	66
Who Wanders Within—The Woman in Question	71
Phantoms of the Opera	77
Who's Loose in the Caboose	85
Her Spirit Speaks to Me	95

I'm **Craig Nehring**. I was born in 1969 in Milwaukee. When I was five, we moved to Minocqua. I graduated from Lakeland Union High school in 1988. At that time my interest in the paranormal began. Friends and I would visit Summerwind, a notorious haunted house not far from Minocqua. When I would see shadows, hear things that I could not explain, watch items move or get tossed, it gave me goosebumps. Nevertheless I became fascinated with the unknown. In 2005 I moved to the Appleton area to start a career in Transportation. I began to watch ghost hunting shows on TV. In time I had my own website and a team of very gifted investigators who would become the Fox Valley Ghost Hunters. We have come along way since then. We have been featured in many newspapers including *The Lakeland Times*, *The Huffington Post* and even a paper in faraway India! My hobbies include fishing, disk golf and my dreams are to someday investigate a haunted castle somewhere in England.

My name is **Jason Ehrhardt**, and I'm from Kaukauna, WI. Ghosts and the paranormal have always been a interest of mine since I was young. I once had a personal experience that kept me asking questions but never getting the answers I needed. I need to know the straight hard facts, and it has me still looking for answers to this day. When I met up with Craig and the team, I knew it was something i wanted to be a part of. I look forward to finding the answers that I have been searching for all my life. I bring to this group my knowledge and experience of various electronics and hope that our investigations can be successful.

I'm **Sheila Heitpas,** and I'm from Kimberly, WI. I have been interested in paranormal activities for as long as I can remember. When I was a kid, my mom and I lived in a duplex. The radio would turn on and the lights would come on seemingly by themselves. One time we heard somebody talking through an answering machine, yet the phone didn't even ring. When we played it back, the message was gone. When I moved out and was living on my own, odd things happened in our house. My son wouldn't sleep in his own room, the dog growled at the ceiling, my washer/dryer doors opened and odd noises went on through the night. After we moved out and a new guy moved in, he claimed he woke up to someone shaking him--yet no one was there. Since then, I met Craig. I thought it would be interesting to go on investigations and be a part of the team.

My name is **Jeremy James,** and I live in Berlin, WI. I've always been interested in the paranormal even as a young child. I never had any personal experiences of my own but always wondered what else could be out there. I keep an open mind and hope to help people who need answers to their paranormal problems.

I have been with the FVGH team now almost from the beginning and have seen so many unexplained things. I think the best part of the investigations is sharing with the client what we have caught and hope to bring more answers to people who have something going on in their homes or business.

I'm **Julia Hebbe**. I am a 20-year-old gal from the Fox Cities. I have had a fair share of unexplainable experiences but never really thought twice about it. I started reading ghost stories, watching ghost hunting shows and of course, "scary movies" at a rather young age. It wasn't until then that I realized how much this stuff really interests me. I am looking forward to being a member of FVGH, I am eager to learn many new things dealing with paranormal activities, equipment, etc. and experiencing everything it has to offer. Well…let's do this!

My name is **Terry Mentz**, more affectionately known as "Bowling Ball" by friends and family. I have been a member of FVGH for about a year and a half. These amazing people are my second family. My primary role has turned into private investigations. I have a military and law enforcement background, and insatiable desire to discover the truth. Not everything that goes bump in the night is paranormal. My background enables me to adapt to situations in many different environments and walks of life. I am a very sociable and empathetic person who can put people more at ease before the investigations start; that is my No. 1 priority. Some houses are very active, some have logical explanations. I view spirits as people who have just shed the shell they were carrying around for years. Each and every investigation, house, person and spirit are unique and must be treated as such. What I enjoy most is the many amazing and wonderful people we meet along the way—some have become lifelong friends. I have a strong Christian background and love to help living people as well as the spirits who need help.

I'm **Rick Seefeldt.** I'm 36 years old with with three awesome kids. I have been interested in the paranormal since I was a youngster. That interest evolved into studying with many parapsychologists, demonologists, plus anything I could get my hands on. I have followed works such as Ed and Lorraine Warren, Hans Holzier and other paranormal authors. My favorite parts of the investigations we do is fact-finding the history and debunking some of the claims--but all of a sudden having that unexplainable moment, like seeing a shadow that makes no sense or hearing a disembodied voice from out of nowhere. I like to not only lighten up situations with my humor, but also try to get my answers (respectfully of course).

I ain't afraid of no ghosts!

My name is **Sierra Diener-Edlund**; I am 35 years old and happily married with five children. I have had a passion for investigating the paranormal since I was very young. As my children played at parks and hung out with friends, my brothers and I shared a passion for cemeteries. Those were our playgrounds. We helped groundskeepers set up and take down flags every year. We also cleaned up garbage and set up knocked-over plants. This was our thing. We respected both the living and the dead. As well as others, I have had my fair share of unexplained things happen in my life .

Hello, my name is **Bri Geer**. I have always been interested in the paranormal and have been working with the team since the summer of 2015. I enjoy learning new things with them. I go places where no one else wants to go, or might be a little apprehensive to go, like a dark corner. Sometimes you will even find me crawling around in crawl spaces to see what I can find. I hope to find more about what is out there and am grateful to have a chance to work with the FVGH team.

I'm **Karri Tessman**. I'm 36 and the mother of two great teenagers. I grew up in Central Wisconsin. I love the outdoors and playing sports. I have been interested in the paranormal since I was a child and experienced things growing up that at the time were unexplainable to me. I have always had the feeling that there is more to life after death...that a spirit or something else can remain. Three different physicians from three different hospitals treating me for three different incidents told me that I must have people watching out for me because I should not be here. It really makes a person think about outside forces that are truly beyond our control. Seeing and hearing things that are out of the "ordinary" have always intrigued me. I look forward to learning more while working with the FVGH team and maybe even helping someone along the way who needs an explanation for what is happening.

I'm **Enid Cleaves**, writer of four books about ghosts and paranormal activities. I grew up in Iola, Wisconsin, worked over thirty years in the Appleton area, earning a B.S—Business Management degree from UW Platteville during that time. I began my writing avocation shortly before retiring to Manitowish Waters. A prospective publisher, who didn't see a market for my humorous cookbook, suggested ghost stories around the Great Lakes as a topic that I might try. I started out as a skeptic, but definitely advanced to the "maybe" stage. The Fox Valley Ghost Hunters have intrigued me; I've been on a couple of their investigations and want to do more. My writing experience includes reporter for my college newspaper, author of a humorous column for a semi-monthly newspaper, field editor for *Country, Country Discoveries* and more currently *Our Wisconsin*. For several years I did assignment writing for the tourist publication *Fun in Wisconsin*. In my spare time, I like outdoor activities such as skiing, snowshoeing, water sports, hiking and bicycling. I also love to play Mah Jongg and other games.

WHAT HIDES IN THE BERLIN TANNERY?

FVGH originally investigated this historic site in November and December of 2011. The 75,000 square-foot structure in Berlin, Wisconsin was built in 1853. While always a tannery, the name was changed in 1892 from Basset Sheepskin Tannery to Sears Hitchcock Tannery. In 1923 a huge fire gutted the building, and all was lost. It was rebuilt and named the Berlin Tannery. It remained in operation until around 1987 when production jobs were transferred overseas. Since that time the foreboding building has been vacant or used for storage and offices for other business. In recent years it has served as a laser tag facility and a haunted building for Halloween tours.

Berlin Tannery today

Did we refer to the tannery as *vacant*? A place so full of history must have some ghosts lurking about! FVGH have identified several of the phantoms here: Sid, Steve, Ed, Megan, Jim and perhaps up to ten others that roam the old tannery. Who *are* these phantoms?

Sid shows himself as an 8-foot-tall shadow. He is a frequent occupant of the tannery who claims he was murdered (but not on the property). Not much is known about Steve. When asked to make himself known by knocking or banging in a certain place, he graciously responds! Ed, or Eddie, is a long-time resident here who, like Steve, is a bit hesitant to provide information about his life. He does like to interact with guests at the tannery, touching them and sometimes even pulling their hair. Megan seems to be attached to a carousel that was in storage in the building's basement. She first appeared there, saying that she was seven years old. A picture taken by the FVGH seemed to indicate that she had long dark hair and dark eyes. Jim is believed to be one of the former owners that had an office on the second floor. Though no deaths have been recorded at the property, it is said that back in the 1950s a human hide was shipped here. Its origin or place of shipment could not be determined.

In the past, two mediums spent time at the tannery. They concluded that there was a portal on the property where spirits enter and leave as they please. Perhaps the non-identified ghosts that visit here are transients or friends of Sid, Steve, Eddie, Megan and Jim!

Haunted tours: "Hallowed Chambers" and "Misery House Incorporated" have been offered at Halloween. Hides hang from the walls, realistic looking but vague enough to suggest that they might be of human origin. "Creatures" step out of their dark shadows, eliciting screams from some of the tourists. Creepy crawly things dangle just above your head, webs brush against your face, and glowing eyes pop out of the darkness.

Waterfalls tumble into a moat; a heavy mist blankets something sinister lingering just below the water's surface. Hallways lead to nowhere. Will guests be able to find their way back to their normal world or will they blend in with other phantoms that may forever call this building home?

Craig asserts that "guests on the tours have been poked, pushed and scratched." Shadows are seen lurking in a corner or crossing a hallway. Sounds are heard of someone walking on the catwalk, yet nobody appears. Craig spoke to that *someone.* "If you don't get back to work, you will all be fired!" *Someone* seemed to be running across the top floor; then a door slammed shut. Meanwhile, the owner of the old tannery heard *someone* run past his office. He peered out onto the main floor and saw nothing. Next, the team heard footsteps approaching them. Shadows blackened the windows, yet there was nothing there. Nothing that could be seen, but *something* very paranormal was at work.

Upstairs view of the Tannery

Craig explained: "We have many EVPs (electronic voice phenomenon); some of them mimic us as we talk. I got lost in one part of the building and forgot my way back. An EVP, sounding like a woman's voice, told me which way to go. It's too bad I couldn't hear her at the time."

Craig talks about "something dark at the tannery."

> One day I got an itch to do another investigation at the Tannery so I called my team members to meet there that evening. My team consisted of Julia, Sheila, Jason, Jeremy, Rick and myself.
>
> We began the investigation by unpacking our equipment and setting up cameras on the upper floors where there seemed to be the most activity. I handed the gals some voice recorders and headed to the second floor to ask some questions. We made our way through the maze left standing from the haunted house attraction back in October. We walked over to an area that is long and narrow that still had some old industrial ceiling fans hanging from the ceiling, which were not working. We began asking questions to see if the friendly ghosts, Ed and Sid, were there and what they were up to that night. We first asked Ed if he could make a noise for us and were greeted with a loud bang, followed by what I believed were footsteps coming from behind us on the stairs we had previously walked up to the second floor. We asked several more questions and heard a floor board creak next to us.
>
> I asked, 'Is that you making the floor boards creak?' I heard that same noise again, only much closer to me. That noise startled me this time, as it seemed to be right on top of me. I switched my flashlight on, illuminating most of the room, but the room was so long that it was hard to see

very far. As I was looking down the corridor, I saw a huge dark shadow. I only saw it for a split second as it shot toward Sheila and Julia, up into the air and out of sight. They were obviously terrified because they screamed through it all. I believe we just saw Sid as he was described to me as the tall dark shadow figure in the tannery.

We spent a little more time in that room, asking them to answer other questions and make some more noises. We heard some knocks and bangs and then decided to go down one more level. There was a maze left over from the Halloween haunted house attraction. We opened a door resembling a cattle chute that slides to the side and walked down a ramp to an open area that several mediums have claimed to be a portal. This portal is said to be in the middle of this room and allows spirits to come and go as they please. This would explain the different ghosts in there from time to time. I placed Sheila and Julia out of sight by themselves. I handed them a K2 meter, which picks up positive and negative electrical energy. I had Rick ask some questions because, for some reason, certain spirits don't seem to appreciate him as much as the rest of us. Rick began when Sheila said she heard a noise really close to them. Sheila then asked the ghost to touch her K2 meter. Almost immediately we heard a loud bang, then Sheila and Julia began screaming while running towards us. I asked them what happened. Sheila stated that not only did someone touch her meter, but grabbed it out of her hand and threw it on the floor. I made sure they were okay and that the meter still worked and then continued our investigation.

We asked a few more questions in the area where this happened and heard some more unexplained noises. We then felt a cold spot creeping up on us. It was so cold, it made us all shiver. You could almost see your breath. It was 75 degrees on that floor, so the cold spot made us believe that something was very close by and wanted to communicate more. It was also lighting up the K2 meters in our hands, which convinced us all that the spirit was still with us. Eventually the cold spots disappeared and things quieted down.

We then decided to move down to another room that we dubbed the echo room because every noise made in that room seems to echo. This room has the most power sources because all of the power from outside enters the building here. The floor, walls and ceiling are made entirely of cement. There are several couches and chairs in this room where the team can sit, relax and listen without having to stand for the entire investigation. I decided to break out the ghost box, which is a device that scans white noise and allows ghosts to talk to us in real time. I turned it on and we heard a couple of the usual voices, like Sid, Ed, and a few others. Something then told us to leave and to run. It is not unusual for us to hear things like this, but it was unusual to hear this at the Tannery.

We continued listening when Julia asked, "Did you hear that?" Then I asked, "Hear what?" She informed us that she heard a loud buzzing noise, but none of the other team members could hear it, including me. We sat there quietly for a little bit when Julia said she now heard a louder noise. However, none of us heard anything out of the ordinary, so we decided to take a break.

When we got down to the main room, I sat down and noticed Julia was not with us. It's not like her to go off into the dark by herself, so Jeremy, Rick and I headed back upstairs to check on her.

When we got back to the same floor where the echo room is located, Julia walked out of the dark room where she heard the buzzing noise and continued down the hallway to a room leading to a former office. She stopped about halfway down the hallway and just stood there looking into the darkness. I asked Rick to see if she was alright. As he approached her, Julia raised her hand up in the air, signaling him to stop. She slowly pointed to the wall and said in a slow deep voice, "He does not like you and wants you to leave."

Rick said that he didn't see anything. Julia again points and says, "Don't you see him? He's right there!" None of us saw anything except a wall at the end of the hallway. Julia then turned around and walked right past us as if she was in some type of hypnotic trance. She kept walking through the break room, but now she was stomping like a mad robot. She walked out the front door, over to her car and just leaned against it. I told Rick and Jeremy to go sage her as she was not acting like herself. After they performed the ritual Julia seemed to become aware of her surrounding, but couldn't remember anything from the time she heard the buzzing sound in the echo room. Julia left for home, visibly shaken.

We have no definitive answers for what happened that night. Some might call it a demonic possession while others would say it was a dark entity that took her over for a short period. I would like to think it was the latter, as there are no demonic entities in the Tannery. This was definitely the most intense thing we have encountered as a team.

We frequently checked on Julia, but she was back to her usual cheerful self and would return to the Tannery many times.

Note

For readers not familiar with the term "saging," here is an abbreviated description of the process: Herbs are used in the clearing and cleaning of both mind and body, thus releasing negative energy.

Pictured to the left is a bundle of white California sage. Latin word for sage is salvia, meaning "to heal."

Our team decided to do another investigation at the Berlin Tannery. I brought Rene, her niece Brittany and nephew Dakota, plus a few of his friends to come along and see what they might encounter. Jeremy, Julia and Rick joined us. After unpacking the equipment, we headed upstairs to what we call the "hooks room" as it was once used to hang animal hides to dry. We began by asking if anyone was there, and thought we heard footsteps come up the stairs. Nobody was there.

I asked a couple more questions. Then I yelled "Marco."

"Polo" came back; we all heard it.

After lingering a while, we headed to a lower level through a sliding door. We stopped at the bottom of the ramp where there was a huge room separated by a lot of walls. It had been used for a recent haunted house tour. We asked more questions and heard some loud knocks come from behind the walls. More footsteps sound like they were heading in our direction; but, again, nothing was visible. The gals seemed a little scared, but we assured them they were fine. We saw some shadows scoot across the hall going down to the next level leading into the echo room (so named because when you talk, there is an echo). Here everything is made of cement.

We took a short break in a room with some old furniture that had been stored here. A few random knocks and noises coming from some corners were heard, but nothing too outstanding. We decided to head down to the basement in hopes of finding more activity.

Old Mustangs (the auto variety), tires, old auto parts, even an old race car belonging to the owner were stored down here. There was a cart with old drywall on it. I had Rene and Brittany sit on the cart to give them a break from standing. Jeremy, Rick and the rest were standing close by when I decided to pull out the ghost box to scan white noise and hopefully talk to the spirits. I asked who was there; nothing intelligible came back. Then, we heard, "Up on the catwalk." Looking at the catwalk, I asked if anyone was there.

"Rick, come up to catwalk." Rick stood up and headed there when there was a loud noise right in front of him. We saw nothing.

I continued to use the ghost box and picked up the word "evil" a few times. We have heard that before; sometimes I think the spirits like to scare us. I asked some more questions. Some different voices could be heard talking. Suddenly a male voice says, '"3,2,1,sleep." In that instant Rene fell forward. I had to stop her from falling off the drywall. She was in a state of sleep and not responding. We all tried calling her name. Rick came down off the catwalk, and we were all yelling for her to wake up. I was afraid that she may have had a seizure as she had some health issues.

That didn't seem that was the case, so I shook her a bit and tapped her face. Suddenly she came to and appeared to be hyperventilating. In addition to having breathing problems, she was shaking from head to foot. We got her up. She asked to go up to the main floor so Brittany and I took her to what we call the "safe room" to help her catch her breath. Now away from the basement, she was feeling better. She would wait for us here while we finished the tour.

We headed back downstairs. Rick said something was talking on the ghost box about sleeping, so I asked if they did that. A voice came back that said "Evil did it." We all knew something had happened, but were unsure what.

We moved from that area to a room just a little further to the end of the tour that leads into another room. We stood in that room for a bit, asking questions. Suddenly, I caught something out of the corner of my eyes. It was a pair of red eyes coming from an area close to the race car. It gave me chills. What was more disturbing is we were not using flashlights. It baffled me that we saw the red eyes without using the lights. Rick got a glimpse too before they disappeared.

We did not walk back that way and decided to call it a night. I wanted to get back to the safe room to check on Rene. She had calmed down and was playing games on her phone.

We had a great night. Our friends left and headed home. I was able to take Rene home. She explained in her words what had happened and what it felt like to her. She heard a voice say "sleep" and then the countdown. At that time it felt like something took control of her body and would not let her wake up. Frightened, she could not move or breathe for a few moments and felt her body shaking. When we got her away from the basement, she returned to normal. Rene said she felt that she was possessed by something in there. I saged her and made sure that she was all right. She continued to accompany us on some of the team's investigations.

Julia investigates the basement of Tannery.

SUMMERWIND BLOWS SPECTERS IN

Emma was born in the early 1920s and lived on the west side of West Bay Lake on the Cisco chain of lakes that lies mainly in Michigan. West Bay Lake dips down into Wisconsin just a few miles west of Land O' Lakes. While in her teens, Emma and her best friend Mary would fish from a rowboat on the lake. She recalled one evening when they noticed ominous dark clouds approaching. The wind picked up, and the girls worried that their boat might flip over in the waves. They started to row hard and fast towards home when they saw a woman on the shore waving them in. Emma described her as tall, very thin, with long flowing blonde hair and wearing a long white gown. The lady pointed towards the house on the hill and beckoned to them to follow her up the hill and into the huge mansion. It was only later that they would come to hear the stories of this mansion known as Summerwind.

Contributed photos:

The lady motioned for them to sit down in the living room; then she headed up the stairs. To their astonishment, she vanished in the middle of the staircase. Frightened, they headed back outside and down the hill to their boat. By this time the rain and wind had calmed down, and they were able to safely navigate back to their home.

Intrigued about what she had seen, Emma called Mary the following morning. The girls decided to visit the mansion again. Approaching the shoreline near the huge home on the hill, they saw the lady once more. She was waving her hands again, this time indicating that they should head away from the shore and go back home.

Everything would seem clear the next day when they learned that danger, or even death, might have befallen them had they visited the mansion that day. A caretaker there had gone crazy and started shooting at people in his sights. No reports were heard of anyone being killed or injured that day, but others have mentioned the lady in white.

Another story that circulated in later years involved Robert P. Lamont. Lamont was Secretary of State under President Herbert Hoover from March 1929 to August 1932. Lamont allegedly hired African-American workers. A caretaker was to pick up several of these workers who were gathered on the opposite side of the lake. Again, there was a terrible storm. Their boat capsized; men drowned. Their bodies were never recovered.

Yet another unverified tale related to Lamont's daughter, Lucy. She asked her father's permission to marry a young man, but he forbid her to do so. Undaunted, Lucy said she would marry him anyway. When Lamont left the mansion, Lucy and a few members of the staff remained behind. It was said that she had an affair with one of the hired help. Her husband found out and told the man to leave the mansion forever. Then, he took his wife to the basement and shackled her to the wall where she was left to die.

There are reports of a female named Lucy buried on the property. The present owners of Summerwind who purchased the property in the mid 1980s were working in the basement of the estate when they discovered shackles driven into the cement of the foundation. This would seem to verify that someone, perhaps Lucy, was imprisoned there.

Note: Various Internet sites list Robert P. Lamont's two daughters as Dorothy and Gertrude. While the name "Lucy" pops up every now and then in stories about Summerwind, we cannot seem to verify that she was Lamont's daughter. Other stories refer to a little girl named Lucy who was buried on the property. A paranormal investigator (not a member of FVGH) reportedly remembers an old stone back in the woods engraved with the then still-legible "Lucy."

Each year the FVGH team heads up to the Summerwind property where the owners have given them exclusive camping rights. In 2012 most of the team was there. The property is back in the woods near the Michigan border and difficult to find. The wilderness here abounds with beautiful wildlife. Deer stop to gaze at you from the edge of the forest; eagles cavort overhead. If you are lucky, you might see a mother bear with a couple of cubs. Hidden among many trees, shrubs and tall grasses are the remains of the mansion. It is difficult to recognize the driveway that leads up a small hill, but when you reach the crest and witness the field stone foundation and massive chimneys, a feeling of awe and mystique overtakes you.

Remains of an old porch where children once played have since been vandalized by young people who partied at the abandoned estate. Peering down into what was once the basement, one can see new pine trees growing amongst the utter chaos of metal sticking up here and there that was once the plumbing and the furnace. Fragrant lilac bushes add to the serenity of the property that belies the violence and destruction of its past.

Craig, Kerri, Jay and Kim arrived and unpacked their equipment and gear, they prepared for two nights of investigating and communicating with the ghosts of

Summerwind. They gathered some wood and started a fire to keep mosquitoes away and provide warmth on a cool summer night. As dusk settled in, it became time to bring out the ghost-box, the device that allows the team to "speak in real time" with the beings that haunt the area. K-2 meters show energy fields, though no electricity is available at Summerwind.

Two members, Kerri and Kim, each holding a K-2 meter, head up to the porch of the foundation that overlooks the lake. West Bay Lake can be seen now only through small spaces between the overgrowth of tree branches.

A member speaks through the ghost-box. "What is your name?"

A reply comes back: "Amy."

"Where are you from?"

"England."

"Do you want us to rebuild at Summerwind?"

"Yes."

Suddenly there is confusion on the ghost box: "Go get them...coming up driveway...get them now."

As the team tries to make some sense of it all, Jay offers to check the driveway. He yelled out; the rest ran to see if he was okay. At that time some kids were seen running down the driveway and into the woods. Apparently, they were trying to steal items from one of the trucks, but the ghost had warned the team of the intruders.

The investigation continued. Suddenly one of the K-2 meters went wild. A voice from the ghost box says "three, two, one" and "go get them—hurry and fast."

In the sudden confusion Craig responds, "This is insane; is someone headed up the driveway again?" The group decides to check it out together. As they rounded the corner near their cars, they saw three guys standing there. Realizing they had been spotted, the three ran off into the woods, dropping their beer cans in the process.

Craig yelled for them to come back, promising not to harm them. About ten minutes later, they would hear one door, then two, and then three slam in the distance. Apparently the intruders had parked further down from the property and were leaving.

Remembering the ghost's warning, Craig believed the ghosts were keeping watch over them. That would be confirmed by the last response they would get that night on the ghost box. A male voice informed, "Little girl dead is your friend."

Craig remembered that he once had a little girl follow him home from Summerwind. "I felt like I was not myself and disconnected from the world." He sought out healing from a shaman in Green Bay who did a Native American healing. "I felt a huge cold spot lift from my body, and the shaman said that was when the little girl left me." At that time they heard the girl say that she needed to stay with Craig because he needed her help. But they told her that she must go because she was making him sick. "I felt better after the healing process, and weeks later I was back to being myself."

A friend of Craig's, a paranormal investigator, had a little girl follow her home from a school. The investigator had said "I have little girls at home," so the spirit wanted to come to her home to play with her girls.

But back to the story.... It was now time to head back to the camp, make some dinner on the fire, and reflect on an interesting day!

That night a noise that sounded like a loud groan awakened Craig. Now awake, and thinking that he had been dreaming, he heard the sound again. One of the team yelled "Did you hear that?"

Craig rewound the recorder and played it back. The recorded voice did not sound like a groan, but more like a voice yelling "Mommy." It became obvious that no one would be getting much sleep that night. Shortly before dawn, more strange noises were heard. A huge shadow passed across the tent wall. Outside was a bear calling her cubs to follow as she exited the camp site and continued on her way.

The next day was spent cleaning up the property and greeting other team members who were just arriving. At dusk a fire was started. Everyone got ready for another night of investigation. This night would prove to be one of the most intense nights at Summerwind!

Craig describes the night:

> Jason, Julia, Sheila and Rick are with me on the front porch of the mansion ruins, standing there while using K-2s and some other meters along with voice recorders. I had tossed a stone down into the foundation only to have something come flying back in my direction. We all heard it. So now we wonder, who or what was tossing stones back at us?
>
> About five seconds later another loud noise sounded next to me...and then another. We had no clue where they were coming from so I walked over to the other side of the foundation to check. While standing there, I heard Jason yell, "'Ouch." He then explained that he was just hit by a small stone that seemed to coming out of the sky outside the foundation.

We brought out a thermal camera to enable us to see through the darkness. Could it appear to be some kids trying to trick us? Apparently not! We then moved to a different side of the building to listen for any noises. Julia and Sheila were now down below the porch.

I heard Julia yell as a pebble hit her hand. She said that she wasn't hurt. Now they were landing all around her. I asked if she would pick them up and show me. They were all very small, about the size of a penny.

I called for everyone to come up and stay together to see if it would happen again. After about three minutes, another pebble came down right in front of me after it bounced off Rick's shoulder. This kept up for about two hours; then suddenly the activity stopped.

We decided that we would put some of the gals in isolation up in the wooded area about 50 yards from the fire. It was near here that a little girl may have been buried long ago.

The rest of us took a break—but not for long! Suddenly we hear both Sheila and Julia scream, so we ran up to see what had happened. They were shaking as they related how a raccoon fell out of the tree and landed right next to them. They decided to move back down by the fire! I pointed the camera at them in case something else happened

As I reviewed what what had been recorded, a voice was heard saying "I pushed it" right after the raccoon landed on the ground. Yikes, I really think some ghost here has a sense of humor.

We sat around the fire for a little while and then decided to head for bed. We had to be up early to leave in the morning. I teasingly threatened to throw marshmallows at the gals' tent so the bears would come again. Maybe the ghost thought it would be funny to toss stones in place of the marshmallows as I had suggested!

Sometime in the middle of the night we all heard screams. Sheila and Julia were yelling that something was striking their tent. I assured them it was not me and told them to take a look out of their tent. After more screams, it was discovered that little stones were being tossed again—but only onto their tent, and from out of nowhere. This went on for about an hour.

We never did find out about the stones being tossed but learned from another paranormal group that the same thing happened to them. We will continue to camp at the property and try to communicate with the ghosts that were there protecting us.

A little more about Summerwind.... In the 1940s it was sold to the Hinshaw family. The ghost sightings did not stop. Shadows appeared in hallways, voices stopped when someone entered a room. An apparition of a woman floated through the mansion. Arnold Hinshaw reportedly found human bones in a crevice behind a closet door. His automobile burst into flames. He became mad and pounded the keys of the piano late at night. His wife Ginger tried to commit suicide.

Ginger's father, Ray Bober, later bought the property but never lived there. They stayed in an RV parked on the grounds. He wrote a book called *The Carver Effect* under the pen name Wolfgang Von Bober. Jonathon Carver was an explorer who Bober said was looking for a land deed that he thought was buried on the property.

Relatives of Bober claim that he made up a lot of what appeared in his book.

Later, the Keefers would own the property. After her husband's death, Lillian Keefer subdivided the land to various buyers.

Summerwind was vacant most of the 1980s. Walter and Berniece Petgas purchased the property in the mid '80s. In June 1988 Summerwind was struck by lightning and burned to the ground. Or, did locals torch it to keep trespassers off the land?

The present owners, Harold and Babs Tracy, would like to rebuild using the original blueprints. A B&B establishment, maybe including a museum, might be down the road—the road leading to what has been referred to as the most haunted place in Wisconsin.

Charles Griffith stands in the ruins of Summerwind.

CRIB IN THE ATTIC

A woman named Megan called Craig one evening to ask if he would check out the farm house that she owned in northeast Wisconsin. She claimed that one night while she was sleeping in her second floor bedroom, she woke up to a noise that sounded like a door sliding or moving. That door was the door to the attic.

What she saw next was incredible! Someone or something had slid the attic door aside and pulled the drapery all the way from the window into the attic as if that someone was cold and wanted a cover for warmth.

Drapery, still connected to the curtain rod,
is pulled into the attic.

Megan went on to say that sometimes she would come home after dark, driving up the driveway past the barn and around to the stables where some of her clients kept their horses. It was here that she saw something white shoot through the barn and quickly disappear. Some of her clients saw it too, claiming it looked like a man running. It was difficult to determine as they would only catch a glimpse of the phenomenon.

When asked if she knew any details about the history of the farm, Megan said one of the hired hands had died there while tending to a bull in the stable. Apparently, the bull charged him and he was impaled by one of the horns. She claimed the blood stains were still on the wall of the barn. Also, there were instances where some of the animals seemed to be led out of the barn by someone at night, yet the security cameras picked up nothing.

When she bought the house, something just did not "feel right." There was a baby crib in an extra attic. That room seemed "creepy" to her. After she moved in, there had been a fire in the house. Though the floors were stable enough to walk on, everything in the house was destroyed—except the crib! It was still in tact, never touched by the fire, even though everything around it was charred.

Bottom of crib in lower left center

Sparked by the picture Megan sent him (no pun intended) and the story about the crib, Craig was excited to begin the investigation. About a week later he pulled into the driveway staring at the blackened two-story farmhouse with all the windows blown out. Remembering Megan's stories, he admitted that the scene "gave me the creeps!" As he looked up towards the attic, and knowing that the crib was still in there, Craig remembers that he "felt chills go up my spine." He rarely investigated a place by himself, but had arrived a little early to "get a layout of the place." Another team member would be joining him soon, yet he felt a bit intimidated being alone. "Something seemed to be calling to me from that window."

The farmhouse was off to one side, while the barn and stables were on the other side, making an L-shaped design. If you were to drive into the barn area, you would get a clear view of the stables with the car lights on at night. There was a huge yard in the back of the house where one could ride the horses. The road was close to the farm, so Craig knew that he would have to account for the noise of traffic during the investigation. Yet it was eerily quiet. There were no other farms or houses close by and only an occasional car made its way down the road past the lonely farmhouse with the crib.

Soon Casey arrived. The two brought their equipment out ready to start the investigation. They knew that it would be difficult to see inside the house at night with its walls blackened from the fire. This would require heavy duty flashlights, similar to spot lights.

The two could "barely see our hands in front of our faces" as they made their way through the various rooms on the first floor. Craig thought he heard a voice behind him, yet wasn't sure. They made their way up to the second floor. The wood under their feet creaked with each step. Craig thought to himself, "I may end up in the basement if these steps aren't secure." To test his safety, he did a few jumps on the first few steps. Soon they were at the top floor. There it was: "The thing that still sends chills up my spine: the curtain hanging in the attic with the door pushed aside. What in the world did this? And why? And WOW!" He reasoned that whatever did this, had to grab the curtain and push the attic door aside just as Megan described.

When they turned on the ghost box to ask questions, the two got an immediate "Hello," then "You need to leave now!" Another voice warned, "Danger."

Craig replied with a question, "Did the ghost start the fire?"

A voice answered "Yes." Sometimes a spirit will tell you what it thinks you want to hear. So whether or not that ghost started the fire—who knows? After a few more questions and some not-so-nice replies, Craig and Casey decided to go see the crib.

Megan had spent a few hours shopping on the day of the fire. When she returned, the house was in flames. There was no baby in the house at the time of the fire. Yet, somehow the crib, unscathed by the fire as though someone was watching over it, seemed to be the focal point of the destructive blaze.

The crib was located in a small subsection of the attic; almost in its own little room. The door leading to this room was so small that the investigators had to crawl on their hands and knees.

Both Casey and Craig asked their respective voice recorders if someone was in there and, if so, could they make a noise. There was no response so Casey asked a few more questions, starting with "Is this your crib?"The real question is which man jumped the highest when a terrible sounding noise like a squeal or growl of some sort was followed by a loud noise next to the crib. They would not have run out of the room if they wanted to; it was just too dangerous because of the weakened structure. In a last ditch effort to get a reaction from the spirit, a piece of burned wood was tossed into the area, but nothing moved or made a noise.

Moving on to another bedroom down the hall, the two were amazed to find a white hand print outlined in the soot-blackend wall. It was as if someone put their hand there while the fire was ravishing the house. The print was small, like a child's. It was a mystery how it really got there.

The two headed downstairs, making their way to the barn and stables. Again, there was a noise on the steps. Craig clearly heard two adjacent stairs creak, right behind him. He turned and asked, "Are you on the stairs with me?"

Later, after reviewing the audio, he discovered that he had captured a voice that said, "I am right behind you."

Outside of the building, the two stopped to gather their wits. They needed to ensure that there was no traffic on the road at the time of that awful growling noise in the room with the crib. They rationalized that the noise could have emanated from an animal inside the house, but yet...there was no sounds or movement until the questions were asked. No more noises were heard coming from that room after that.

Old blood stains still stood out framed by a white wall inside one of the barn stalls. What secrets would that stall have to tell? As they came around a corner, a light shot out of one of the stables. It may have been an orb, but Craig admitted that "it could also have been my eyes playing tricks on me." Nothing audible was picked up here. After four hours, the two decided to call it a night. They would go over the audio the next day.

The recordings revealed what sounded like a little girl's voice saying she was in the room with the crib and that she was very cold. Would the curtain have warmed her? The other audible noise, sounding like a moo from a cow, came from the barn. No animals were seen in the vicinity of the barn. According to Megan, a cow did die in the barn while giving birth. This was moosic to their ears; it would be the first animal that the FVGH ever captured on their audio equipment. Other paranormal groups, however, have said that they have recorded animal noises on their equipment.

Megan asked if the FVGH could do a clearing on the house. Craig called a shaman from Green Bay who arrived the next week. The woman began the cleansing and healing process. A fire was started in the back yard. This was to remove anything negative in case Megan wanted to rebuild.

The shaman also wanted to help anyone who might be trapped here to "cross over." According to Craig, this refers to the spirits "physically moving from the earthly plane to heaven or another realm where their loved ones are." Prayers were said and old rituals used to bless the land.

Suddenly, out of the clear blue sky a lone, iconic bird cast its shadow across the flames of the fire. This majestic bird was a bald eagle, the sign of freedom and peace. It was signaling that the cleansing was complete and peace would be restored to the property.

Megan has since bulldozed the property. There has been no more known paranormal activity since the property was blessed.

GHOSTS VACATION AT GREENVILLE STATION

Greenville, Wisconsin, located in Outagamie County, is one of eighteen communities that make up the Fox Cities, the third largest metropolitan area in the state.

The Joseph Kronser Hotel and Saloon was built in Greenville in 1887, but later destroyed by a fire. Kronser rebuilt the hotel ten years later. The large two-story building was used as a railroad hotel, with a ticket office and five bedrooms. It was the social center of Greenville. Several different owners ran the hotel until 1934 when it became an Oldsmobile, Chevrolet and Studebaker dealership. After 1945 it changed hands again and served as a barber shop, bus station, funeral parlor and a fire dispatch station. Food was served at the station for many years; various road crews ate here.

In 1988 Kevin and Tina O'Shea bought the building and restored it to its appearance at the turn of the century. The Greenville Station was a popular restaurant in the late 1900s. Wedding receptions and other functions were held in the upstairs ballroom. Finally, it was closed and reopened in April 2012 as Bootleggers.

During the short time it was open (it closed again in autumn of 2014) there was a long list of downright spooky and potentially dangerous encounters with spirits from the past.

Greenville Station, a.k.a. Bootleggers

The Sheas told many stories. One of their waiters was walking down the hall leading to the kitchen when "something" smacked him in the face so violently that his glasses flew off his face. The waitresses would hear bangs and knocks as well as voices in the bathrooms during times they were sure that nobody was in the building.

The owners themselves were petrified of going down into the basement and would descend down the old wooden stairs only when they absolutely had to—like when they were out of beer or ice.

From the kitchen old wooden stairs lead down to a room that once contained an old coal furnace. Further back is another room used for storage. Hallways at the bottom of the stairs leading both to the left and to the right appear to be cut into the old stone wall. In one place, hidden in the wall, is another staircase. A few coolers and compressors are still stored in the area.

Amidst the dark, dank and dreary maze of rooms, and behind a door that had been nailed shut by the bartenders, there is a small area with a dirt-covered floor, matted down with high and low spots. It could appear as if someone had been buried there—maybe hurriedly. One could almost visualize a person trying to cover up the shovel marks by stomping on the ground with his feet. Next to that was still another small room with a sink--perfect to wash up, before leaving the body to eternity. If cobwebs could talk, there might be a lot of stories.

Around the corner are more stairs leading into more creepy narrow halls leading to more dark, dank rooms, some with dirt floors. While in the basement the owners would hear noises as if something was sliding across the floor. Voices came out of nowhere sending them racing up the stairs. But these goings-on were not only in the basement. Lights in the bar area would flicker, and objects moved around by themselves.

What possessed Rick?

The FVGH visited Bootleggers five times and have amazing stories from each visit. Craig relates one story that was "totally off the charts." It was in the fall of 2014. The owners had closed the bar early so the investigators would have free range of the building. As the team readied their equipment in the bar area just to the left of a couple of pool tables, Terry and Sheila were sitting on stools next to Craig.

Suddenly, Terry jumped up, Sheila let out a small yelp and Craig felt a breeze rush by him. It seems something brushed Terry's leg at the same time it pinched Sheila's leg and then blew by Craig. The reality of the incident appeared as a reddish mark on Sheila's thigh. We didn't even have all of our equipment ready, yet stuff was happening," Craig recalled. The night had just begun!

Adjacent to the pool tables is a hallway leading back to a kitchen, and another hallway leading to a banquet room. Large functions, such as wedding dances, took place in the larger banquet room upstairs.

By now the team had readied their equipment and were ready to roll. The first step was for the team to listen for noises in the upstairs banquet room. Then they began to ask questions, hoping for responses from whomever or whatever lurked in the old train station.

Non-musical sounds come from the room today.

Suddenly, a loud noise exploded from the hallway just outside of the banquet room. Sheila screamed; the pinching phantom had struck again. Meters on their equipment started to detonate; an affirmation that something else was with them in the room.

Soon all calmed down. The group decided to regroup! Terry and Rick would stay by the pool tables. Sheila and Julia headed down into the basement. As Craig sat on the steps, the women walked a bit further into the basement. It was truly pitch black down here and quiet enough to hear a pin drop. Then the gals started to ask questions. An answer came--in the form of a punch to Julia's side--as a loud noise broke the silence and footsteps seemed to be following them as they ran for the stairs. Their screams cut through the darkness like a sword. "I yelled for them to stop," Craig recalled, "but they almost ran me over in the process of going up the stairs." He joined them on the main floor. They were shaking; Julia was holding her side in pain."

While the gals finally calmed down, the guys headed downstairs to try to try to communicate with what was down there. "Why would you punch a woman?" Craig then followed up with, "You better not harm anyone else; that was NOT nice."

The response was a loud noise. Then a pipe that had been sitting against the wall literally and forcefully hit Craig's leg, cutting it open. "I know for a fact the pipe was leaning at enough angle that it could not have fallen by itself." Craig continued, "We headed back upstairs. My sock was turning red, and I needed to stop the bleeding."

The pain dissipated, and the team was ready to get back to work. About that time the owners and a waitress came in. They were asked to join in, reluctantly agreed, and the whole group went back downstairs, most likely with a "safety in numbers" mind set.

In the basement again, they dispersed and quietly waited for whatever would happen next. In just a few moments footsteps were heard on the wooden floor above, near the pool tables. The footsteps seemed to approach the basement door, and then stopped. Then, there was a loud noise, deep within the basement and again, it was Julia who, this time, had her hair grabbed and pulled. The waitress, who had experienced weird happenings in the past, felt something rub the back of her shoulder. She was done, went back upstairs and left the building!

Next, everyone heard a voice say, "Over here...." The activity seemed to end, and the team decided to call it a night and head upstairs. As they were packing up their equipment, Craig wandered off to the bathrooms for some final questions. In the ladies room he heard a woman's voice that was later confirmed on the audio, saying "Watch the children."

More noises, knocks and bangs were revealed when the audio equipment was reviewed. At the time the pipe hit Craig's leg, "It was me" seemed indicate a confession. What sounded like a horse running in he distance made some sense, as this place was a railroad station in the day when horses were tied up outside.

Greenville Station is still closed and for sale as of this writing. The team loves this place, and offers public tours here as well as overnight investigations.

PHANTOMS FROLIC ON FRANKLIN STREET

This investigation was conducted by Terry, aka: Bowling Ball, and Jane at a private residence on Franklin Street in Appleton on November 14, 2014. A call was placed to Craig by a woman named Laura who had just purchased the house and was in the process of remodeling it before she, her 13-year-old daughter, and her long-time boyfriend would call this their home.

While cleaning and making necessary repairs before moving in to her new house, Laura heard crying coming from the downstairs bedroom. She also heard doors rattling, someone walking upstairs, and a radio playing (even though there was no radio in the house.) When she stepped outside, she could not hear it. Laura informed Craig that a contractor had been hired to paint the interior of the house before she moved in. The painters heard crying in the downstairs bedroom as well. "I'm not afraid of spirits, Laura related, but I want to know what's going on in my house—and why!"

Jane, FVGHs' chief historical investigator, did some research on the house hoping to reveal any pertinent information. Her findings were as follows. (Names have been changed in respect for individuals' privacy.)

> The house house was built in 1950. Jim and Eleanor Smith lived there with their two daughters, Susan and Betty. Eleanor passed away in their home on November 9, 1959 of a heart attack. Jim remarried Laura Jones. We were unable to find a wedding date, but there was a birth announcement for their son Andy on August 22, 1961. Jim and

Laura were already married as the mother's name is listed as Laura Jones. Laura's first husband died on November 8, 1957 (two years before Eleanor's death). They had two children, Mary and Isaiah. Jim and Eleanor's daughter, Susan, died May 30, 1963 at 13 yrs old. The other daughter, Betty had a baby named Elizabeth who died as an infant. Cause of death is unknown.

On November 14, 2014, Terry and Jane arrived at this address to do a private paranormal investigation. As requested by the client, they arrived at approximately 8 p.m. Approaching the front of the residence, the two could see through a big picture window into the living room. Laura had a big smile on her face and waved to come in. Jane opened the front door and stepped into the living room. "I felt like my heart was going to explode," Jane lamented, "It was such an extreme feeling of sorrow; it was all I could do to keep from crying. Terry added, "I would like to note that I am a United States veteran and a former police officer, so I have seen more than my fair share of sorrow and horror, but nothing had prepared me for this."

Nevertheless, Jane walked in smiling and immediately began talking. Laura, her daughter and Laura 's friend were sitting in the living room. Laura said that her best friend would be coming after work. They all wanted to sit there while the team did their investigation. Jane warned that they could sit there, and "as long as they were as quiet as church mice, it would be no problem!"

Laura related things that had gone on since she purchased this house. She said that this would actually be the first night they stayed there. After chatting for about 45 minutes, the team began setting up their equipment and turning off anything that would produce unwanted noise, such as the furnace, dehumidifier, etc. After the equipment was set up, Jane walked throughout the house taking reference pictures. This is done in the event that something is captured on the camera or video throughout the investigation, it can be compared to the base pictures.

Jane started on the main floor which consisted of a living room, kitchen, bathroom, dining room and what might be considered a sun room without furniture. One wall had windows, a door leading outside and a fire place on the end. Jane stood in the doorway to this room taking pictures. Suddenly, the flash on her camera went off, and the shadow detector in the basement starting beeping. She remembers thinking, "Wow! That thing is sensitive!" Then she turned to take a picture down the stairs to the basement, which is directly across from the doorway to the sun room. The shadow detector did not go off this time. Although unable to see the shadow detector, she turned the camera in its general direction and shot off another picture. It still did not make a sound.

"Interesting," Jane thought; then walked down the hallway. She related to Laura what had just happened. "She found that equally as interesting." Laura then asked her "if she could feel the sorrow that I felt." Jane informed her that she had felt it as they pulled up in front of the house."

Jane then went down into the basement to take pictures. All the while, she felt someone watching her "although I did not feel threatened or anxious in any way."

She took some more pictures upstairs while talking to Laura's daughter, Mary. Apparently, the daughter had experienced no paranormal experiences in the house, but her mom and the painters did. She also said that she and her friends like to play with the Ouija board. Craig offered up his professional opinion about the board, trying not to sound like a parent. "I pray it did not fall on deaf ears."

The two then went through the house with their electromagnetic field (EMF) meters that affect the behavior of charged objects near the vicinity of the meter. An EMF is produced by electrically charged objects such as wiring, any electronic device, humans and spirits. One of the main reasons for this scanning is to make sure that the occupants of the home were not affected. An unusually high EMF can cause feelings of being watched, and even hallucinations and bouts of depression. This particular house had unusually low EMF readings.

In his own words, Terry reported on their investigation that evening:

> The average outlet or light switch is about 2 milligauss and a breaker box is about 20 miligauss. We tried using several different meters to verify they were working properly. It's worth noting we did not get any abnormal EMF readings. About 9:40 p.m. we began our investigation in one of the upstairs bedrooms. We started doing an electronic voice phenomenon (EVP)) session in an effort to communicate with any spirits that may have been in the room. Eventually we heard a couple of unexplained noises. Then, while I was sitting with my back against the wall with the door to my right, I thought I heard a light knock. I saw the door slowly open approximately 6-8 inches. We invited whoever was at the door to come in and talk to us. The door began closing about three times as fast as it opened. Jane then said, "I feel compelled to go to the other side," (meaning the other bedroom). I said that I did too. So I said out loud to the spirit, "OK, we'll come into the other room and talk to you." Later while listening to EVPs, we heard a female voice say, "Thank you." We went into the other upstairs bedroom and began an EVP session. We heard a couple of unexplained knocks but could not verify the origin.

A couple of minutes into it, we both heard a disembodied female voice, but we could not understand what it said. So we decided to use a ghost box to try to communicate.

One of the questions Jane asked was, "Did someone make you cry?" We heard a voice but couldn't understand what was said. So Jane asked the same question. Listening to EVPs later, we captured a female voice saying, "My husband." We continued asking questions after turning on the Ovilus. We continued with the EVP session for a little while longer but didn't really hear anything audible at that time. Jane took another baseline EMF reading but found nothing unusual.

We then went back downstairs to take a break. I went into the bathroom. As I stood in front of the toilet, I slowly turned around and opened the shower curtain. I swear someone was in there but it was empty. Jane and Laura both told me later that they have the same feelings in there.

We went into the basement for the next part of our investigation. Jane shined the flashlight down the stairs during the walk down, and the shadow detector did not make a sound. While we walked through the basement, Jane said something just touched her head. I turned on my flashlight and looked at the ceiling and it was clean as a whistle. A couple minutes later, Jane said she felt something touch her head again. I walked around taking pictures in the dark while Jane did another EMF baseline reading. She couldn't get any baseline readings, even though the temperature meter was working. I began walking around with my EMF meter and got the same results; no baseline readings. We decided to move on with the investigation. As we were walking into the main part of the basement, I felt what I thought was a spider web on my head. I turned on my flashlight and the ceiling was clean. Not a spider web to be seen anywhere. Jane said she had the feeling a few times.

We then sat down and began an EVP session. We asked whoever was down there to say something or make a noise. We heard a couple knocks but could not confirm the origin. After a period of time with seemingly no communication, we decided to set a mag light over in the corner of the basement where we heard the knocks and began a yes-or-no EVP session. We asked the spirit if it was able to turn on the flashlight. We waited about a minute after I sat down, and the light came on by itself. So, now we began using that as our method of communication. We told the spirit to turn the light on if the answer is yes and leave it alone if the answer is no.

Jane heard a whisper in her ear at the beginning of the session but was unable to make out what it said. Some of the questions we asked received a "yes" answer, indicated by the flashlight turning on by itself: "Do you want to talk to us?" "Is there more than one spirit that lives here?" "Do you like being here?" During this time, we heard a loud bang on the floor above us. It literally sounded like someone had fallen off the couch. The women upstairs did not hear that noise but informed me they heard walking upstairs. We heard that noise later while listening to EVPs. "Do you know what the person that cries is upset about?" "Is the person who is sad usually down here in the basement?" "Is the person who is sad the one walking around upstairs right now?" "Does the sad person want to tell us something?" Then we heard that loud bang above us again. "Do you like the sad person?" "Does the sad person want to stay here?" (The EVPs picked up disembodied voices.)

"Is the sad person named Eleanor?" These are just some of the questions we asked and got responses in return. There were some questions we got no responses from as well, so we are assuming those answers were no.

Jane felt something tap her head four or five times while we were in the basement. One of the questions we asked that got a positive response from the flashlight was, "Are you touching her on the head because you like her?" We then went back upstairs to the main floor to take a break and let the women take a break. We sat and talked for over an hour getting to know everyone. One of the best things about private investigations is meeting some amazing people like Laura, her daughter and her friends. We will be friends for the rest of our lives. While I was sitting on the couch, I could see into the kitchen doorway. All I could see of the kitchen was the top cupboard, the microwave, and the cupboard beneath it. On the door of the microwave, I could see the little green light of the ice maker on the refrigerator located on the opposite side of the kitchen from the microwave. I saw the green light go off for a second and then come back on as Laura said, "I just saw something move, like just right through that door. "

Right after she said that, a voice responded, "No shit!" Laura then started giggling. I saw the little green light go out again for about a second and then come right back on. I got up and walked into the kitchen. Whatever was there seemed to have disappeared. Later, while we were talking, I went back into the kitchen because I thought I saw a shadow go in there. Laura then said she thought she just saw something, and Jane said she just saw something go around by the steps.

We decided this would be a good time to go into the bedroom, the final room in our investigation. We had set up a full-spectrum camera at the beginning of the investigation. When we went into the bedroom, it was off. I got that extremely sorrowful feeling again walking into that bedroom. Jane got the camera going again and we sat down on the floor. Since we had success in the basement, we decided to put the flashlight out again and began an EVP session. We didn't get any responses for about the first 15-20 minutes. Then the flashlight came on by itself when we asked if Eleanor was upstairs. Some of the questions we asked in the bedroom with a positive response were: "Are you a man?" "Are you the one we saw in the kitchen?" "Does Eleanor go in the basement?" "Is Eleanor on this floor?" We heard some unidentified noises in that room. It sounded like someone walking above us but we couldn't confirm that. All of the women in the living room were sitting quietly.

Jane's EMF meter was going off like crazy for a couple minutes. We decided to use the Ovilus and the ghost box again. We couldn't confirm anything coming from both, so we shut off the Ovilus. Again, we asked for a name, and "Michael" came over the ghost box. I asked if it was Michael who said to turn the flashlight on. The flashlight then turned on with no one near it. We asked the spirit to turn the flashlight off, and it went off instantly. When we asked where Eleanor is right now, we got a voice over the ghost box saying, "Under the …?" We listened to the EVP at minimum of fifty times and could not make out the last word.

That's one frustrating part of reviewing evidence; sometimes you can hear a voice but never figure out what was said. We continued our EVP session for a little while longer. By now it was 3:15 a.m.

and we knew we had enough evidence to know there was definitely more than one spirit in this house. I finally said to Jane, 'I'm just gonna come out with it." Then I said into the ghost box, "Since Eleanor is unable to talk to us or doesn't want to, is she sad about her husband, and what he did? A voice came from the ghost box, "Maybe." Listening to EVPs later, we noticed that a couple seconds after that response from the ghost box, we captured an EVP that said "Bye!" Everything seemed to go quiet after that. We sat there a little while longer and decided to wrap up the investigation. I turned the ghost box off, and we got up and started to gather our equipment. As Jane shut the camera off, we heard a rapid succession of three or four knocks on the wall. We thanked the spirit for making that noise. Later, listening to the EVPs, we were wrapping up the cords to the cameras when we heard a crystal clear "Thank you!"

We went back into the living room to let the women know we were done and then gather the rest of our equipment. I went upstairs to get the camera and the voice recorder that we had left for the duration of the investigation. I noticed that the voice recorder had shut off after a little over four hours, although there was still approximately 2/3 of the battery life left. I then turned around and closed the door except for about the last four or five inches. I then tapped on it with my finger to try to reproduce the door opening and closing, as a small draft can cause some doors to seemingly open or close on its own. The door did not move.

We then said our goodbyes and talked about this amazing investigation all the way to our respective homes, knowing full well it would not be the last time we were at this house.

ANYTHING GOES AT OLD ST. JOES

Craig Nehring described the St. Joseph Catholic church that caught his interest when he moved to Berlin in 2010. Located on the top of a hill, it could be seen from anywhere in town, towering above the trees. The place of worship was massive, made of granite stones from a local quarry, with a cross that reached toward the heavens.

St. Joseph church, school and living quarters

There were about eight churches in town. Some, like this one, were closed. One day Craig saw a truck in the driveway and decided to stop. He recalls, "It was the owner who collects churches—or at least owned two of them already. I told him I had admired his church from everywhere in town." Of course, Craig's next question was if the owner thought the building was haunted.

The owner replied. "I've heard footsteps coming toward me and then stop. It scares me to think that something or someone is walking around in there."

Within no time a date was set for two weeks hence for the FVGH team to investigate the church.

Craig, Jeremy, Daphne, Rick and Kim were given a tour of the many buildings on the complex. The first, a yellow brick one-story building contained many bedrooms, all the same size. This was the nuns' quarters. The adjacent two-story building with large granite bricks was the priests' quarters, or rectory. There were several bedrooms on different floor and staircases on both sides. However, only one staircase led to the cellar with its many rooms. One room contained newspaper clippings from the early 1930s.

View from the pulpit

The next building was a huge church with two floors and a balcony. The stained glass windows were beautiful to behold. A basement with an old tin ceiling once was a dance and stage area where children would put on plays. A hallway from the main part of the church led to several classrooms, each with chalkboards. Here the nuns taught the kids who were all dressed alike in their school garments. At the end of all the classrooms was a staircase that led down to a small gymnasium. There were no basketball hoops, and the room appeared to be too small for basketball. Perhaps other games were played in the room.

That concluded the tour. The investigation would begin in the nuns' quarters. The quiet and serenity here would end quickly! A voice came through the Craig's hand-held radio sounding like "messenger." The other radio was not yet turned on, but members of the team all heard the transmission.

It was on to the rectory. Some questions were asked. Suddenly, loud clanking noises emanating from the second floor disrupted the questioning. Hurriedly, Craig asked the ghost box who it was that they were contacting. A voice replied, "Father Fiss." It was learned later that this priest was killed in a train-car accident. A couple more questions were asked with no responses. One of the investigators felt something burning on her arm. There were some small raised scratches on her wrist that were red but not bleeding. This incident left her "a little freaked out."

The team continued on, heading upstairs to the second level where most of the bedrooms were located. Here, they heard more loud noises. A team member captured a shadow darting into the room, disappearing into the floor of a bedroom. The room turned cold; indicating something was surely there. A voice recorder was left on that floor while the team continued onto the attic.

A heavy presence was felt in the attic, almost suffocating in nature. A response on the ghost box to a question asking if anyone was in the attic came back loud and clear: "I am."

"What is your name and how long have you been here?"

"Gabe...I have always been here at St. Joseph Church."

"What do you mean you have always been here?"

"Before earth and before time." The voice then became silent.

Craig remembers the moment well. "If that didn't send shivers up our spines, nothing else would! We could not put a finger on it, but something seemed like it was not right about the attic and what was up there."

The team went back down to the level below the attic. Looking up the attic stairs, one team member courageously yelled, "I don't believe you are here; prove you are really up there." As quick as the words came out, the presence approached the team. Loud "clopping" steps were heard coming down the stairs. Investigators ran from that area of the attic. The team member who asked for proof was very quiet after that!

They headed into the darkest area in the building—the basement. The invisible "presence" followed. Stairs creaked behind, yet nothing or nobody could be seen.

The equipment then picked up an unintelligible voice. Footsteps were then heard overhead; but when the team got to the main floor, they had stopped. The voice recorder was then reviewed to see if anything had been captured while the team was exploring elsewhere. A raspy voice muttered, "Get out." The recorder was left on as the team headed to the church.

The team took seats in the pews inside the massive room with the high ceiling. A response over the two-way radio, "Messenger," was heard again by all. Believing that maybe something was trying to send a message by identifying itself in that manner, the team waited a little longer. Nothing more was heard so they headed down to the basement (ballroom/stage area).

Here shadows were seen moving in the doorway and footsteps heard approaching—but then stopped. The team continued up to the school area and sat down in a classrooms. Doors were heard slamming, and voices interrupted the silence of the dark room. It was then that Craig "heard something I have only heard one time before. That was someone playing basketball in the gym." The sound stopped as they reached the last step on the stairs leading to the gymnasium. Nobody was there, yet Daphne felt a scratch on her back. Upon viewing, the area was raised and red, but disappeared quickly.

Pictures taken in the girls' bathroom seemed to all to show a little girl drinking out of the fountain.

The team decided to call it a night, but decided to ask the owner if they could do some tours there. He said, "Sure...and handed us a key." When Craig arrived at his home, he realized that he forgot the voice recorder. Luckily, he now had a key and retrieved it the next day--a bit apprehensively however.

"I wanted to get in and out as fast as I could and not be there by myself." He went right back home to see if the voice recorder captured anything. Footsteps were heard going up and down the stairs all night after everyone had left the building.

"I decided that I was never going in there alone again." Craig continued, "Tours would be intense; guests were often scared before leaving the first floor." Guests continue to talk of the paranormal, telling stories of their encounters here.

Craig remembers one tour exceptionally well as being "very scary. There is always more than one investigator on a tour—for very good reason. This particular tour consisted of about ten guests with three investigators. Craig brought up the rear of the group "to make sure it went smoothly." Kim and Tara were leading the tour with Jeremy close behind. The tour began in the church, and ended in the staircase to the gym.

Craig was trying a new thermal image camera to try to capture hot and cold spots of people in the frame that are invisible, but with a heat signature. People at the top of the staircase were asking questions; Craig was pointing the equipment towards them. Tara suddenly looked really scared and called to Kim saying she was unable to move and that something was holding her there. As Craig pointed the thermal towards Tara, Kim pulled her away from the wall. Craig saw what appeared to be an unidentifiable shape, but as Kim pulled Tara away from the wall, an image moved away from Tara's body and disappeared into the wall.

Craig shudders, "I told Kim to go sage her. We continued with the tour and almost got it done when Kim came and got me--so I had Jeremy finish. I went back to our main quarters (the nuns area). Kim said that when they went to grab some sage from under the table where it was stored, something growled at them in a nasty voice. Tara was outside and in tears." She said she was never coming back here.

Tara continued to do other investigations with many good results. She and Kim did return to St. Joseph's Church after about a year to do one last tour. It was a good tour for both of them.

The FVGH no longer investigate this place as new caretakers have taken over. Their privacy continues to be respected.

INSIDE THE WALLS OF THE FIRST WARD SCHOOL

Existing schools in Wisconsin Rapids were overcrowded in the late 1800s. A new state-of-the-art school was in the planning stage. It would be heated by coal but equipped with electricity and would incorporate all of the latest technology including venetian blinds, high quality blackboards and adjustable seats.

Bricks for the building were made on site. All four large classrooms were painted with watercolors. The 17,000-square-foot three-story structure, situated on two acres of land, was completed in 1896 to educate Kindergarten through Grade 6 students.

In 1902 the school was named the Irving School after the popular author, Washington Irving. In 1910 the bell tower was destroyed by lightening and never replaced due to the cost to keep it running.

Later, due to the increase in students, the school was used for students only through the third grade. The teachers here now were nuns; their quarters were in the attic. The nuns began to experience strange happenings at the school. Supposedly they kept a log of these activities, but it was never found.

A fire occurred in 1921 when embers from the coal furnace ignited the roof. The janitor, returning from lunch, discovered the fire and was able to evacuate the children. The roof was soon repaired.

A small area in the school would be used to teach the deaf; and another would host the first special education classes in the city. In 1954 a kitchen and cafeteria (that doubled as a gymnasium) were added, bathrooms were moved from the basement, and the coal furnace was converted to gas. In 1977 the grade school was replaced by offices and classrooms for exceptional students.

First Ward School: 2015

In 1979 the building was abandoned; well, almost. The caretaker, Oscar, Betty, Miss Holliday and perhaps others still live here, along with a real present-day, very-much-alive person: Justin Libigs.

In December 2010 Libigs' family (Justin, his mom, stepdad, daughter, uncle, aunt and cousin) purchased the old school. They all seem to have a penchant for experiencing psychic phenomena. Justin remembers conversations he had with his Grandfather Bert when he was five years old. (Bert had passed away before Justin was born.) By the time Justin was in third grade, he was delving into the paranormal world, reading books on the subject. At age 12, armed with a Polaroid camera and a cassette recorder, Justin went on his first investigation at a local VFW building.

Today, he is a paranormal investigator, author, lecturer, tour guide and originator of "Relatively Haunted," a project that studies how close-knit family bonding can have an effect on paranormal activities. Justin believes that "ghosts respond and react more readily with people who are comfortable with each other," and that the "ghost is a peer—as opposed to an experiment."

With his "Ghosts are just people—eternal human souls" belief, Justin asserts that his best interactions with spirits are when he is not investigating but conversing, including and interacting with them as "just people."

Social functions and parties are popular here. Rather than trying to tell a spirit what to say or do, they find they get more reaction by interaction. At Christmas stockings are hung for the children, gifts given and old records played.

Betty asked for a blue bicycle. Maybe that is what she was riding when, as a kindergarten student, she was struck and killed by a hit-and-run driver back in 1934.

"You don't have to die at a place to inhabit it," Justin explains. "Parents always told their children to go to a safe place." He reasons that the "safest place she [Betty] could find was the school." Betty seemed to be sad at first. Voice recorders picked up "I only want to go home." Now, she is happy. In fact, recently they saw her "clear as day" dressed in a pretty plaid frock...and smiling!

A realtor showed the building to Justin and his mother, Carol. A former principal, Miss Holliday, greeted the trio in her rather formal sounding, high-pitched voice, "Hello." For over three years, nobody knew the voice was that of Miss Holliday. Surviving relatives shed light on the subject. "Oh, she is still here." Turns out, the principal had previously offered her name, but it was interpreted as the definition of a "holiday," such as

Christmas or Easter! Miss Holliday shared space at the old nurses' office (now a bedroom). Doors here often close, probably by Miss Holliday.

A little boy named Oscar attended school here. He had some disabilities and was often ridiculed and bullied. This school was one of the first to offer students like Oscar a place to obtain an education. One day, Oscar purportedly was found hanging in the attic. Did bullies accidentally kill him? Did he commit suicide? During this (World War I) era, suicide was a disgrace. Also, the bullies may have been children of local rich and prestigious families. There were no documents. Was it a coverup? Did this tragedy really happen, or did the energy from many people who talked about the incident manifest here?

Spirits of other children could reside here as well. There is a closet at the back of a classroom where students were allegedly placed for misbehaving. Stories circulate that one child was forgotten there until discovered about 10:30 p.m. An EVP was recorded of a little boy saying "I didn't do it." Later, a visiting psychic heard the same words. Knocks on the closed door are heard frequently.

Once a classroom, now used for conferences, seminars, etc.

Children visiting here sometimes see apparitions. An eight-year-old boy, touring with his family, saw a little girl peering from a window and waving to him. His family could not see the apparition.

One four-year-old boy told his mother he saw a man in one of the rooms. When Mom asked what he looked like, the boy described him as wearing green pants and a green shirt. Maybe it was the caretaker?

The caretaker, who has appeared in black and white, is said to have been an alcoholic who had been given a chance to work here. He taught young boys how to play basketball. He seemed to be popular with his peers and superiors. Yet, was it all as it seemed?

Women seldom held positions of authority back in those days (exception: Miss Holliday). Certain types of work were considered "man's work." The caretaker had that attitude, it seems. He doesn't treat women with respect. Just ask Justin's mother.

Mom was cleaning up the basement after an event, picking up candy wrappers from the floor. As she stood up, she felt two hands on her chest, pushing her back against the brick wall. She estimated she was held there for about five seconds, although it seemed like five minutes. The force released her, and she ran up the stairs—never to return to the basement again. In fact, she won't go anywhere in the house alone. Now, when she visits, she sleeps in a recreational vehicle parked outside the building.

The aforementioned real estate agent was pushed into the opposite side of this brick wall. Those instances, plus the abundance of shadowy figures and the belief that this spot may be a portal from the spirit world into the building, makes this area a very active one. Also, stories have been told about molestations occurring in the small room under the steps here. Strangely, there is a lock on the *inside* of that cubby-hole room.

THE wall—Libigs believes may be a portal for spirits

Neighbors have reported strange lights emanating from the windows at night. One claimed to have seen an elderly man near a third-floor window. There are those who hear the sounds of a little girl crying.

Some of the adjacent neighborhood sits on top of what used to be an old cemetery. To allow for a new housing development, many (but not all!) bodies were moved to a different location. Some graves did not have tombstones, Some people were buried in a pine boxes. They did the best they could, yet human bones were said to have been unearthed with the building and renovations of the old school house.

When Libigs bought the property, he was pleased to find very little vandalism--only one room, on the second floor, had graffiti on the walls. The lavatories were all in tact, internal school bells still rang, and a couple of boxes of coal remained in the basement, though the building had been converted to gas heat. His family soon got to work. Voice recorders were used to make notes about the repairs, etc. When Libigs' stepfather checked out the windows and suggested replacements, a voice retorted, "Just leave them." While his mom and aunt were on the second floor complaining what a mess it was in, "No it's not" came back!

Second floor bedroom often used by over-night investigators

The oldest surviving school in Wood County has been repainted, furnished with period furniture like the bedroom set shown above once owned by a rich family from St. Louis, the couch set on the next page, and a chest of drawers that once belonged to a mass murderer. One would never notice that the bottom of the chest contained a concealed drawer— the drawer that held his tools of trade.

This place is not what you would expect from a "haunted house," but more of a modern-era museum with some amazing relics, mementos, art work, antique furniture and period furnishings--plus some invisible "tour guides!"

Craig and Justin on a couch once owned by friends of Al Capone

As a parting note, Justin remarked about the spirits that abide within his abode: Footsteps, disembodied voices, and a few objects getting pushed around. Basically, "Ghosts are respectful. Tell them to keep the noise down and they will." As a final note, he added, "They are just like roommates, but better 'cause they don't eat my food!"

FVGH Investigation

So much has been said about the First Ward School; so many investigators have captured so many incidents. The FVGH wanted to see the place for themselves. They would do a two-night investigation.

Justin met them at the door, then gave them a tour with some great stories of the spiritual residents. Then they were free to wander and check out the building before starting their investigation.

The team noted that the first floor had classrooms with big black chalkboards, teacher's desks, kids' tables and chairs, as well as toys and objects scattered throughout the room.

The second floor classrooms would offer beds for the team to sleep that night. Craig remembered thinking "how inviting this place was to stay," even if they would not be investigating.

Because of the unique structure of the attic beams, this level is believed to have been constructed by the Freemasons. It was one of the largest attics Craig had ever seen. The staircases, one on each side of the attic, lead down to the basement.

There they noted a room with chairs, a projector and screen for presentations or seminars. On the other side of the basement they walked through a few small rooms, the furnace room, a coal room. At the lower level they discovered a small kitchen with a stove, refrigerator, popcorn machine and hot dog machine--all of the conveniences; they would not have to leave the building.

The team set up their equipment and started their investigation. Sheila and Julia were in the basement to take pictures. Craig and Rick were stationed on the second floor.

After about fifteen minutes, screams brought the two men running down the stairs. Sheila had witnessed something in the dark move "really fast" near the coal room. A scarey Halloween prop was swinging back and forth, though nothing apparent seemed to set it in motion.

Emotions were more calm now, and the four set up chairs in the small windowless coal room. While Craig asked if "Oscar was down there," the Rem-Pod went off and approaching footsteps were heard. Then, Sheila felt something scratch her hand. Upon investigation "they found a couple of marks there, one spouting a little blood, but nothing serious." Apparently, this type of thing happens frequently on investigations.

There were more noises and knocks. A review of the voice recorder picked up a voice of a girl saying, "This is Betty."

"Wow, very cool to hear from her given the history of her spirit being tied to the school." The team adjourned to the kitchen for a break. On their way a small rock or piece of wood flew out of the projection room and hit Jeremy on the shoulder. They quickly walked into the room, but found nothing.

After the break, the group headed to the attic. Here, "things quickly took on a life of their own." Loud knocks, footsteps coming up to the top of the staircase, then stopping, a loud thump followed by the sound of a breath of air coming from the unseen force.

"I then felt something touch my neck and face," Craig related. "I decided at that time to turn the ghost box on and ask it if someone had touched me."

A male voice came back, "Sorry for touching your face."

"Confirmation that someone indeed touched me; how cool was that?"

It was getting late; the team decided to get some sleep. A voice recorder left on all night revealed noises and footsteps that were not their own!

The next day was spent going over events of the evening before. Later in the day, the team resumed their investigations.

Terry went to the attic as he wanted to do his own investigating there. The rest headed to a classroom where they read stories and played with Tinker Toys, hopefully to get some reaction from the kids.

"I want to play," came a young girl's voice.

A few knocks came from the punishment closet.

Meanwhile, in the attic, Terry decided to ask some questions of Oscar. At that time, "a bright white light appeared, danced around the room and landed in a bucket on the other side of the room." A quick check of the bucket showed it to be empty. Perhaps it was just Oscar, announcing his presence in the unfinished room that will someday be the First Ward penthouse.

It was late; the team headed to their beds for a few hours of sleep before returning to their homes to analyze the information from their audio and video instrumentation.

The team continues to have some "really great nights there" and has returned many times. Now, once a year, they invite the public to spend the night with them investigating the active classrooms, halls, nooks and crannies of Wisconsin Rapids' old First Ward School.

GHOSTS STIEHL STALK THE WINERY

Wisconsin's oldest licensed winery, Von Stiehl Winery in Algoma, Wisconsin is housed in a building erected during the Civil War and listed in the National Register of Historic Places.

von Stiehl Winery

In 1868 the Ahnapee Beer Brewery established a brewery here. Henry Schmiling (great-great-great-great uncle of the current winery owners, Aric and Brad Schmiling) became the second owner of the Ahnapee Beer Brewery in 1879. The brewery closed in 1886 due to a severe hops blight and was used for storage, as a feed mill and a washing machine factory. By the 1960s it was in disrepair.

Dr. Charles Stiehl purchased the building in 1964 when it became evident to him that he had outgrown his cherry wine making business housed in the basement of his home. Dr. Stiehl asked the state to grant him a winery license and began making wine from Door County apples and cherries. He soon patented a wine wrap of gauze and a mixture of paint and plaster of Paris to protect the wine from heat and light.

Dr. Stiehl sold the winery to Bill and Sandy Schmiling in 1981. In 2003 they turned it over to sons Aric and Brad.

Henry Schmiling still hangs around the winery. A former employee, Jim, saw him peering out of the fourth-floor storage room as he finished a tour outside the building. Another former employe, Edye, tells of the time she was helping to clean before a major event at the winery. While mopping floors in the basement, she heard the sound of a dinner bell. Knowing there were no bells in the basement, Edye addressed the bell ringer. "Im a little hard of hearing. If you want me to have dinner with you, you'll have to ring the bell a little louder." The bell rang loudly. "Henry heard me, "Edye quipped.

A lot more goes on in the winery. An apparition has been spotted in the restrooms at closing time. Wastebaskets holding the doors open are found moved the next morning and the doors closed. Rocks are sometimes found inside the building. Keys, as well as clothing, have disappeared from an employe's desk drawer. A half empty beer can was found on a step leading down to the basement. Strange things happen near the closed tunnels in the basement. Workers trying to find out if extending a tunnel might be viable found a cross of seven stones in front of the hole when they returned to work the next morning.

The tales go on and on. Many believe that there are other ghosts besides Henry who may reside here.

After reading an article in the newspaper about the winery doing a ghost mystery and wine tasting event,

Craig decided to call and ask if the FVGH could do an investigation. Brad Schmiling readily accepted the offer, talking briefly about the ghosts that he believed resided in the building.

It would be a two-night investigation; the first night in the winery, the second in the production plant across the street. Former team members Don, Daphne, Kerri and Kim joined Craig and Jason on the first floor of the winery building. Hearing footsteps above them, Don set up a video camera in the second floor while the rest of team headed down the spiral staircase to the cellar. Here was a large room with dining tables and chairs for events and wine tastings.

Random questions were asked through the ghost box; a few "yes' and "no" responses came back. Despite some loud knocks, bangs, and a few footsteps, the night was relatively quiet. They decided to call it a short night.

Don captured the team's first shadow—one of a person in the office clearly jumping into the viewing area of the camera and then back out again. It was astonishing!

The following night the team headed across the street to the production plant. According to Craig, the aroma of the aging wines in the building was so wonderful that he "just wanted to take a straw and start sampling!"

Aging can be wonderful!

The building consists of the loading dock where cases of wine sit on pallets waiting to be loaded onto a truck. More cases were stored in an adjacent room. Upstairs there is a long hallway with a stairway at both ends and many rooms on both sides of the building. Each room was small, with a single light bulb hanging down from the ceiling. The wall paper was varied, some with faded red cherries, another with big yellow flowers of an unidentified species. Reportedly, the building was a brothel in years gone by.

As team members were setting up their equipment, one of the gals "starts barking out orders to our team." As she headed up the stairs, she yelled, "This is going to be a great night."

She is gone for quite a while, so a team member goes to see if she is okay. They both come down, and head for the door. "I have to leave for a bit." Without any reason given, the two left the building. As the team continued to set up the cameras in different rooms, they both returned.

"She needs to be saged."

Something negative had taken over the investigator's body and mind leaving her with terrifying thoughts. After the ritual the woman proceeded to tell that, while possessed, she seemed to believe that she should take the team to the Algoma lighthouse and drown them all.

(Note: At the time the woman did not want others to know of her chilling event. She is no longer a member of the FVGH, but we honor her request to remain anonymous.)

The investigation continued. Lights from the street crept into the pitch-black rooms. Suddenly, a thunderous crack penetrated the silence. It seemed to have come from an adjacent room.

A light from the ceiling in that room was still swinging back and forth as if someone had swatted it really hard--but who? And why? Soon the momentum was lost; it never happened again.

Craig and the team members headed back to their respective positions in chosen rooms. Unfortunately, the noises and the footsteps came from rooms other than those that were occupied--until Craig heard a creak in the floor sounding like it came from right next to him. Then another sound--from the nearby floor board.

"Am I doing something to make you mad?"

"Mad" was scarcely out of Craig's mouth when the door next to where he was sitting slammed shut, missing his shoulder by inches. The force was so great that the warped door was now wedged in the frame. It was quite difficult to open it again.

By now the team had been summoned to this room. Craig related the story and the camera was inspected. Unfortunately, the door was just out of line of sight with the camera. A bit shaken, Craig told the team that the force of the door could have severely injured him. Who would want to harm him, and why?

Asking the ghost box if someone had just slammed the door elicited the terse response, "Yes, I slammed it." Unfortunately, the perpetrator did not provide his name. Unintelligible female voices came through, but nothing made sense.

So the team headed for the basement, an area with mostly dirt floors. Nothing was seen here, yet something reached out and touched a couple of the investigators.

After a short stay in the storage room, the team gathered their equipment and started packing it into the back of the car. One final odd event occurred. A roll of tar paper that was leaning firmly against a wall in a corner suddenly fell over toward the group.

When asked, the owner said that roll had been in the same position for years. Nobody could determine how or why it suddenly fell over.

Craig summarized their visit at the von Stiehl Winery:

> We went over the audio and captured many voices and heard some footsteps. The cherry on top of the cream was the shadow that was caught the first night.
>
> We all love the winery. The owners are awesome, and we hope to return in the future for more haunts--as well as the great wine they sell there!

Great selection of wines at von Stiehl Winery.

THE SECRETS OF STEVENSON CREEK

All that remains of an isolated three-story building back in the woods is the foundation and a massive 40-foot chimney. Stairs lead into the basement where a few artifacts are scattered. High grasses and trees do an excellent job of hiding the mysterious ruins from view. Logging and snowmobile trails crisscross the area located just east of Highway M a few miles south of Boulder Junction.

Trees now tower over the Stevenson chimney.

People from the Boulder Junction area remember stories about the Arthur Stevenson family. They moved to the area and built a three-story mansion on about 2,500 acres of property. Here they lived from approximately 1905 to 1911, hoping to make a good living by damming up the creek running through the marshy area and growing cranberries. Loggers had taken most of the trees in the area;it is difficult for one to imagine how the trees and brush have grown so tall since that time. Pallette Lake, just east of the foundation, cannot be seen from the chimney today.

Named after the family, Stevenson Creek winds east and then south into Trout Lake. A large sawmill existed on the west side of Highway M near where the ranger station sits today; the rail line went by the mill as far as Pallette and Escanaba Lakes.

Then one day everyone who lived in the house allegedly just disappeared, including the parents and their four children. The house was left abandoned, along with personal belongings and their vehicles. Nobody knows why the people left or where they went.

Some say the cranberry business was not a lucrative one for the Stevensons, that the land was not good for growing the tart red berries due to the irregular terrain and poor drainage. Also, there was speculation as to whether Stevenson knew anything about running a cranberry business. Assuming their endeavor failed, and they moved on to make a living somewhere else, why would the family simply abandon the vast property and their showcase home?

Though people said that Stevenson came from a family who had made a lot of money in the banking business, why did he build such a large and stately mansion where its elegance could only be viewed from afar...and then just suddenly leave?

The state bought the property years later, allegedly for $10 an acre, but really didn't know what to do with it. Campers frequented the place, so did kids looking for a good party or the excitement of a haunted house! The state finally tore it down the home for its massive logs.

In later years people visiting the ruins claim to see ghosts of children going in and out of the foundation. Others see the youngsters playing in nearby Stevenson Creek and running through the tall grasses. There will be windy spots on a calm day.

Still, there remains a lot of unanswered questions.

Craig and a friend, Chuck, visited the Stevenson Creek chimney on July 10, 2011 and "did a quick investigation before swarms of mosquitoes carried us away!" While they were there, Craig asked if the kids liked to play by the creek. A voice, or a noise of a child came back saying "Ah...." A three-word sentence was heard on the EVPs, but it was not intelligible.

At times the men both thought that they heard children laughing. Simultaneously, they would turn to each other and ask, "Did you hear that?" It was like "surround sound"; they were uncertain what direction the voices came from.

Returning from the marsh (where the children seem to enjoy themselves) to the foundation of the house, Craig remembers that he got "this eerie feeling of someone watching us. The chills ran up my spine."

The wind would come and go in strange patterns. "We had a hard time knowing which way the wind was coming from. We could not help but notice all the debris was confined to the foundation, and nothing else was around or even scattered anywhere at all."

They noticed remains of a foundation of what may have been a garage, about 50 yards from the house. The two walked down what "could have been a service driveway for some power poles, and possibly another driveway." But, before getting too far from their car, they stopped. Craig quipped, "I was concerned about being eaten by a bear so we did not go far from the foundation."

Voice recorder in hand, the two decided to leave the premises. Craig tried to step across a muddy ditch, but didn't quite make it. His foot and shoe were sucked into the mud.

When he had time to go over the voice recordings, he heard a voice that was captured at the backside of the foundation saying, "Over here." As Chuck discovered a plastic box aside a brick, a voice remarked, "big spider." (Was there a spider in the box?) The last utterance on the recorder occurred when Craig stepped in the mud. It was an expletive!

"Hmm--he might have thought it was *funny* that I stepped in the mud."

Craig returned to the area a couple of times. One particular day he, Kerri and Jay were exploring in the dark. "There was this heaviness in the air choking us. We managed to walk about 20 feet from the car, and off in the distance we heard a growl. All of us can attest that we did not think it came from an animal...but something more sinister." The trio left.

Today, some people hike back in the woods to enjoy the mystique of the ruins hoping to find clues to the paranormal world. Others search for clues to either a geocache or a letterbox. (One of which was found in the foundation by Chuck as mentioned above.)

The traditional geocache utilizes GPS coordinates that lead the searcher to a hidden container. Inside, there will be a log book and often an item for trade. There are many types of geocaches; information and directions can be accessed on www.geocache.com.

Letterboxing is an older "treasure hunt" game. It also involves a container that usually contains a log book and hand-carved rubber stamp/ink pad. Finders make an imprint of the stamp in a personal log book and leave an imprint of their personal stamp in return.

There are approximately 90,000 letterboxes hidden in North America with clues of their whereabouts on their website. Both a geocache and a letterbox are hidden at the site of the Stevenson Creek chimney.

Local trio finds letterbox and geocache,
but no skeletons.

WHO WANDERS WITHIN-- THE WOMAN IN QUESTION

Julie sounded frantic on the phone. Her sister Emily was having problems in the duplex she rented in the Oshkosh area. She had been dragged down the steps by an unseen force. Something scratched her while she was taking a shower. Pictures had been tossed off the shelves and lay shattered on the floor.

This sounded serious. Craig was working, but he called Rick and Jason to head over to the duplex to do an initial investigation. Here they were met by Julie, Emily, Emily's boyfriend Tyler, and their pet black lab.

Rick took some pictures. Then the two tried to get a feel for what had been happening. It didn't take long for them to find out. First it was the strange unidentifiable noises. Then, suddenly, Emily was thrown up against the wall--by whom or what, and why?

After the incident, nothing more happened. Rick and Jason headed home and called Craig.

"This is much more than we bargained," Craig responded after being debriefed. "We may need some outside help." He called a friend, Becky, who is a nurse. The two would meet with Julie and Emily the next day.

Rick and Jason joined Craig and Becky on the ride to Oshkosh. "I need to show you something," Rick asserted as he pulled out the pictures he had taken the day before.

There was a picture of Julie, Emily and Jason seated around the kitchen table. Everything in the picture seemed crystal clear--except for Emily's face. The distorted and disfigured image was unnerving.

"It looked like a picture from the movie *The Ring,*" Craig remembered, where the victim was pushed down a well, died seven days later in the well, then created a cursed videotape showing her deformed face to indicate to viewers the misery she suffered during her life. The viewer of the tape would have seven days to show the tape to someone else or become another victim.

Could this gruesome picture be a camera malfunction? It would seem not, as the other pictures taken had all turned out fine. Becky checked Emily over to make sure that she was not injured from her prior abuse. Meanwhile, the FVGH team members set up their equipment. The bi-level duplex consisted of a kitchen and living room area on the first floor with a carpeted stairway leading to the bedrooms, bath and storage area on the lower level. They took out their voice recorders and a Rem-Pod (that creates its own electromagnetic field and, if something comes near, will emit a warning signal).

Emily and Julie were sitting on the living room couch with the dog lying on the floor in front of them. Craig, Rick and Jason were sitting about 50 feet from them on the living room floor. Becky was on the staircase leading downstairs. The Rem-Pod was located on the lower floor between Emily's bedroom and the stairs.

"Why are you here," Craig questioned, "and why are you hurting this person?" Then he asked for the spirit to give a sign that it was indeed there.

The Rem-Pod went off; Becky screamed that she felt a hand on her back trying to push her down the stairs. Craig felt a breeze go past him. Then, Emily was tossed off the couch by the same invisible force that pushed her before. Shaken, but alert, she allowed Becky to again check her vitals. All seemed to be good.

"Do you want to step out for a bit while we continue to investigate?"

"I'm all right and will stay," Emily replied.

The team entered Emily's bedroom. Rick suggested reading passages from the Bible. Craig did a chosen reading suggested by a pastor regarding Satan being cast out and sent back to hell by Jesus.

About half way through the reading, Emily (who was standing next to her bed) was raised up and again tossed against the wall. Unharmed, but frightened, she began to cry. Why was this malevolent spirit targeting her? Would she ever be safe?

Craig, questioning whether their investigation was adding fuel to the fire, decided to leave. Rick and Jason would stay the night to do the best they could to ensure Emily's safety, though there was no indication that she was the only target (as evidenced by Becky being attacked as well).

About 2 a.m. Craig received a call. "They were talking fast; I told them to slow down and tell me what happened."

Emily and Tyler were asleep when they awoke to a loud noise and screams. Then the door slammed shut and could not be opened for several minutes. When it finally was opened, Emily was crying. Tyler explained that something tried to grab Emily and pull her under the bed while he was hanging on to her with all his might.

Everyone decided to leave the house. Craig promised he would contact a friend, a priest from Indiana, in the morning. Michael does freelance exorcisms. To further explain, he has his own group outside of the church that he teaches and thus does not need permission from the church to do exorcisms. (It sometimes can take months to get that permission).

Michael agreed to set up a meeting with Julie and Emily the next day. He would be staying in town for a few days. He went on to say that he wanted the FVGH team there when he returned to document events that might unfold.

"I believe that it is not only the house that is haunted, but that Emily is also possessed." An exorcism was planned for two days hence.

Michael was already there; Julie and Emily were sitting on the couch when Craig, Rick and Jason arrived. A stranger was setting up a video camera. Craig readied his video camera to record the events as well.

With Holy water in hand, Michael began to read

passages from the Bible to Emily. After several minutes Emily's eyes suddenly rolled back in her head and she began convulsing. Michael asked the guys to hold her down as her body was contorting back and forth. Julie assisted, as the 110-lb. Emily became this combatant monster with incredible strength.

Michael continued to read. Only the whites of Emily's eyes could be seen. "It was like a zombie movie," Craig remembered.

Next, Michael spoke emphatically, "I command you in the name of the Father and Son and Holy Ghost to give me your name."

Emily writhed and wrestled. A voice from her mouth, but not her own, answered the command. "I do not serve you."

Michael repeatedly asked for a name; but one was never given. "You must leave this body and return to where you came from," the priest ordered.

The ordeal seemed to be over when Emily collapsed, crying and hugging her sister. Suddenly, a sinister laugh emanated from her contorted mouth as she reached for Julie's neck. Emily's eyes rolled back again as she mocked those who were trying to help her.

Michael continued to read from the Bible, stronger passages now, meant to reach the possessed woman. After about twenty minutes, she collapsed again, crying. She was tired, and she wanted to sleep.

It was finally over. A calmness filled the room. Julie

held her sister while everyone stayed to ensure that all was well.

In the weeks to follow Emily fought fatigue. At times she felt that maybe she was slipping back into the terrible person that unwittingly inhabited her body. Michael returned one more time to promote some follow-up healing.

A year later--all is well, though ghostly episodes still occur at the home. Rick and Jason befriended the two women and watch over their well being.

Craig deleted the video. "It was something that I never really wanted to see again...it was so scary, something you would only expect to see in horror movies. Yet, things like this do happen in this world. It's a rare occurrence that investigators don't often come in contact with. I'm happy for that, and would be even happier if it NEVER happened again."

PHANTOMS OF THE OPERA

The Grand Opera House (aka, The Grand) in Oshkosh, built in 1883, was indeed grand with its Victorian design, hand painted drop curtain, ceiling and wall completed by local artist, Frank Waldo. The official capacity, including jump seats at the end of rows and in the walls, offered theater goers a choice of about 1,000 seats. Crowds poured in for the opening production of "The Bohemian Girl" on August 9 of that year.

The theater went through a series of owners and names from The Grand Opera House to Civic Theater (then a movie theater) to The Grand Theater in 1950. By the 1960 the building had fallen into disrepair. A "Save The Grand" committee worked for twenty years trying to pass a referendum. Then, The City of Oshkosh acquired, restored and expanded the building using modern materials and methods yet preserving as much of the originality as possible. Work started in 1982, and an adjacent property was purchased. Today, that piece of property is the main entrance to the theater complex.

On October 3, 1986 The Grand Theater opened its doors again, with a new rendition of "The Bohemian Girl."

Serious structural issues were discovered in early 2009 and the building was closed for emergency repair that February. Scheduled performances were moved to alternative venues throughout the city. The Opera

House Foundation initiated a "Stand with the Grand" committee that succeeded in collecting many large "Grand for the Grand" donations. On September 16, 2010, The Grand opened its doors once again, this time with singer Jeff Daniels entertaining at a gala opening. The theater provided free entertainment throughout the following week to thank the community for their support.

On the corner of High Avenue and Market Street

Today The Grand has a seating capacity of 650 and offers approximately 100 live performances each year. Many of the theatergoers are unaware of the "other" performances.

Periods of remodeling or renovation often bring out the *phantoms* of the opera, so to speak. A film crew from

U.W.--Oshkosh was working on the production of a movie inside The Grand. Several of the students saw an apparition of a man with small round glasses smiling at them from the balcony. The man fit the description of Percy Keene, a stage hand here for over 70 years (1895-1967).

A Hollywood producer, Bob Jacobs, was making a fictional movie about a haunted theater, filming inside The Grand. An assistant was hoisted above the theater by a rope, suspended there for about an hour while they shot the scene. As he was lowered down, the rope broke as he hit the floor, with seemingly nothing pulling it to cause the break. The producer concluded that the man had been held at the top by something, or someone else.

Apparitions were seen in an underground passage. A female producer felt someone grab her by the ankle. Other workers saw an apparition in the orchestra pit.

At a private screening prior to the film release, Jacobs saw the man people described as Percy Keene, again smiling down from the balcony. A cinematographer, passing the building at night, saw the same smiling face peering from an upstairs window.

As time went on, more stories began to surface. Staff members told stories of lights going on and off, sudden temperature drops and footsteps on the staircase to the balcony. A dog, once used to patrol the theater, is sometimes heard barking in the basement. A headless man in Shakespearean costume in the balcony and a woman in Victorian dress standing in the aisle are among the visions reported. In 1996 researchers recorded a glowing image crossing the stage. Reports of tunnels leading into the building that may have been passageways for show girls during the speakeasy days, remnants of underground shops, and maybe even portals for spirits to enter--who knows?

The Fox Valley Ghost Hunters visited The Grand Opera House in December 2015. One of their goals had been to do an investigation here, and now The Grand's website offered the theater for rental to paranormal investigators. A telephone call to Events Manager Shawna Terry sealed the deal. They would have six hours to wander through the grand old Grand!

The team this night consisted of Craig, Jeremy, Rick, Sierra, Sheila and Bri, along with former investigators Kerri and Jay. Employees of The Grand would first give the team a tour, starting by climbing the steps to the upper balcony and then to the attic "that was up like five staircases and was very hot." Craig made a mental note not to spend time in the attic. Besides, there was no reported activity there. Why would *any* ghost want to spend time alone in an uncomfortable attic, when it could be down on stage or at least where the action is!

The group then headed down to the balcony and then to the stage area. It was amazing to stand on the same stage that once hosted name performers from all over the country.

Performers such as Harry Houdini, John Phillip Sousa, Samuel Clemons, Charlie Chaplin and Vincent Price—and later stars such as Hal Holbrook, Debby Reynolds and the Smothers Brothers would grace the The Grand's stage.

Enid's late husband, Bob, performed there too with his folk group, Crystal River Trio, along with other members of Green Apple (Green Bay/Appleton) Folk Society. It was a dream come true for Bob, who raved about the fabulous acoustics.

From the stage the group looked out over the many rows of seats with lighting in each row. The balcony extended around the sides, with VIP seating along the edges.

A view from the stage

In the basement below the stage a front section of flooring is stored. It can be raised for a seating section directly below the stage for a group such as a symphony orchestra. The process is completely done by hand, no automatic assistance whatsoever.

There are two ways to the basement: one a spiral staircase, the other "just stairs." Here were several dressing rooms "with so many lights that one would almost need sunglasses." Voices and footsteps are often heard under corridors and sections beneath the stage.

"Some parts had a ceiling so low that we had to watch our step so we didn't bang our heads on sprinkler pipes," Craig recalled. The basement was filled with a lot of chairs and "tons of old props from movies and stuff."

It was time for the investigation to start. The gals would go up to the balcony; the guys would stay on the stage. K-2s and meters were placed in both areas. Craig would alternate between both areas to synchronize, coordinate and compare questions to the responses or other detection of paranormal presence.

About ten minutes had passed. Craig was sitting on a step between the stage and balcony. A loud noise, like a foot stomping, occurred on the step next to where he was sitting.

"What is your name?"

"Percy," came back loud and clear on the audio review. Craig could only assume that Mr. Keene was on the step next to him.

During the next hour noises sounding like footsteps and some knocks were heard in the balcony, but the group was unable to locate what they were or where they came from.

Meanwhile, from on the stage, shadows were seen darting back and forth between the chairs inside of the doors leading into the theater area. The group from the balcony came down to join those on stage.

Then, a woman's scream was heard. Craig rewound the voice recorder; it definitely confirmed the scream.

"We listened some more, and all of us heard some loud noises in the balcony and saw some shadows moving about. We tried to debunk them as car lights, but the lights of the cars were not at that level."

Just maybe, former performers and stage hands were preparing for their evening performance.

Craig yelled,"The show must go on!" An unintelligible reply came back. Playback of the voice recorder picked up "Damn it." Maybe the originator was angry with the intrusion of their preparation or rehearsal.

Research in the basement returned little. "The K-2s were going crazy from all the electricity down there." So they were brought back to the stage area.

Craig and Jeremy went to the basement without the K-2s. As they ventured into a dark corner, Craig started to ask if something or somebody was there.

"I heard what sounded like a voice whisper to me, yet it startled me--I almost jumped on Jeremy."

Jeremy heard it too, but couldn't distinguish what was whispered. Playback from their recorder produced "Go up." It would seem like the ghost did not like having them downstairs and requested them to return upstairs.

That was not going to happen—yet. In fact, Kerri and Jay joined the two since nothing noteworthy was happening upstairs. They stayed on one end of the basement, while Craig and Jeremy walked to the other side.

Craig asked several questions, one of them being "Can you pull on my pants leg?" This was meant as a request to show the group that something was, indeed, down there with them. Nothing happened.

Shortly after, they rewound the voice recorder to listen. A voice said "Of course I can pull your pants leg." (After all, the question only asked "can you," not "will you!")

Another scream was heard, sounding like it came from upstairs. The audio equipment revealed it was the same voice as was captured earlier on the stage.

More doors seemed to be banging, but the origination of the noise could not be determined.

The team packed up their gear and headed home. It had been a long night--but an interesting one--in a very intriguing place! It was a Grand experience!

WHO'S LOOSE IN THE CABOOSE

The National Railroad Museum—It would be something different from the usual haunted schools, churches and factories! Most of the FVGH team agreed, and they were off to Green Bay, Wisconsin. This would be their final investigation of 2015.

New members, Peter and Karri, and former members Kerri and Jay, joined Rick, Jeremy and Craig in their quest to investigate a haunted museum.

Museum Executive Director Jacqueline Frank, along with a few members of her staff, enthusiastically greeted the group and began the tour.

First, there was the Dwight D. Eisenhower train. She explained that during World War II "this was the fastest type of passenger train, and it was the type of train used for General Eisenhower during the war. It was his mobile command center."

Next she showed them The Pullman, Big Boy, and one unnamed electric train. Some of these trains were actually at rest in their present railroad beds when the immense building was constructed around them. "The Railroad comes through the middle of the house...." The lyrics of an old song comes to mind *(Middle of the House* by Vaughn Monroe, 1956).

It's cold outside in Green Bay in December, so the tour was concentrated indoors. Ghosts probably feel the same way! The team split up into different areas. After about an hour, they would assigned to different cars. The summaries below cover the team's experiences in each area during the three shift changes.

Dwight D. Eisenhower

Kerri (Kerri with the "e") and Jay would spend time in this unique train that arrived at the museum in 1964. President Eisenhower visited the train later that year. There was no perceived ghostly activity in this area. The two went outside where all was calm in the cold crisp winter air as well.

The sleek and shiny Dwight Eisenhower

Craig, Rick and Karri (Karri with the "a") came in for the "second shift." They entered the first compartment behind the engine. The war strategy room was furnished with tables and chairs. The hallway (aisle) continued past many windows; sleeping rooms and bathrooms were off to the side. Craig sat down in one of the compartments. A small sign instructed how to use the dial to control the steam heat from the engine. Small lights were tucked into the wall enabling a traveler to read in the dark.

Strategy Room

The rooms were very stylish for a World War II era train. "I could easily be comfortable in one of those beds," Craig contemplated. As a compromise to his thoughts, he sat down on one and listened to loud knocks and thumps—and, "was that a train whistle?" Rick and Karri heard footsteps behind them in the aisle.

As the trio headed for the last car, Kerri and Jay came back to talk with them. They reported that they went outdoors after spending an uneventful hour in the

Eisenhower. All was calm.

As they were comparing notes, Jay felt something push on the back of his kneecap causing him to buckle and catch his balance.

The five team members then headed towards the last room in the Eisenhower. Doors slammed shut as if someone was trying to say, "Do Not Enter." In their analysis of whether the door could close by itself, the group decided that the door had to be opened to a certain point for that be a possibility. It could not be determined whether this was a paranormal activity or not.

There were a few more knocks and noises. The floor creaked as it seemed that footsteps were approaching. Nothing more occurred. Maybe they would revisit the Eisenhower later that night.

On their way over to the cabooses, Craig met with Peter and Jeremy who also had stepped outside for awhile. They reiterated all was quiet out there, and they were happy to come in out of the cold to start their (third) shift here in the Eisenhower.

While in this car, the two would hear footsteps. As you will read in upcoming paragraphs, Peter and Jeremy leave this car, and Karri enters by herself armed with a voice recorder.

As predicted, she did not stay long. Something touched her hand and she heard something walk up to her as well. In ten minutes she was back. Craig and Jeremy decided to check out the car one last time.

By now, the two are the last ones on the train. Halfway down the aisle they heard some loud noises and a piercing scream coming from inside the next car back. Inside that car the K-2 "lit up like crazy." The two looked for power sources that would indicate another source besides paranormal, but could find none.

More questions were asked. Another woman's scream... right behind the men. Could it be the same woman they had heard in the orange caboose? (See following section on cabooses.)

Jeremy's K-2 meter continued to go off in certain cars. Craig called out the window for Rick to come in and verify what was happening.

The three stood in a dark hallway "where you can't see your hand in front of your face." As the K-2 meter went off again, Craig heard an unintelligible whisper in his ear followed by a much louder voice. A door swung half way closed and got stuck on Craig's foot.

A playback on the audio revealed a voice saying "ouch." Was that comment in reference to the door incident? Another voice makes an interesting acknowledgment, "Door don't close all the way."

As they listen a bit more, Rick saw something dart out of a dimly lit room down the hall. A voice replay picked up "You're right," agreeing that Rick saw something.

More footsteps...approaching...stops directly in front of the three. Then a hand is placed on Craig's shoulder and moves him out of the way, as if he was blocking the aisle. Jeremy and Rick escaped into nearby rooms, not wanting to experience the same thing.

Pullman

Craig, Karri, and Rick headed to the Pullman, with its comfortable furnishings, often used for overnight travel. While the latter two sat in a seat a few rows back, Craig sat down on a bed. All three heard voices coming down the aisle. Craig uttered that no-fail word he often uses when trying to communicate with ghosts: "Marco."

A crystal-clear voice came back on the recorder: "Polo." Then the ghost added, "Leave my place." Did he think that the team moved in to inhabit his car?

"What is your age," Craig inquired.

"Sixty (or sixteen?) came back.

Craig moved from the bed to a few rows behind Karri. They heard sounds like someone tapping on the wall and someone walking down the aisle.

A suitcase, used as a prop, was on the seat opposite Craig. Then, Craig felt "someone" sit down next to him and place a hand on his leg. He remained quiet. "Is someone sitting next to me?" he asked. No response....

Give me a wide berth!

Drink..or sink

Cabooses

Jeremy and Peter would investigate some of the cabooses, those freight-train cars used by the train crew and usually attached to the rear of the string of cars. The smell of perfume and fresh logs on a fire were experienced in two respective caboose cars. The two then moved on to the Big Boy. (Nothing was written about events happening in this train, because there were no paranormal activities here to report.)

Craig, Rick and Karri headed to the cabooses. The orange caboose once tipped off the tracks into a river. Luckily, the conductor was able to get out. There was a little red caboose and an early 1900s dining car.

The first stop would be at the orange caboose--a very nice car with a small wood stove. Craig is thinking, "Wow...very cozy," while visions of sleeping danced in his head. But sleep would have to come later.

Craig left the two other investigators and headed to the red caboose. He had "this crazy feeling that someone was watching me," so he set up the Rem-Pod to see if someone would touch it. Although nothing seemed to happen, a later review of the audio indicated a female voice answered "Yes" to Craig's question "Can you touch it?" Nothing on the equipment indicated that she *did* touch it. (Maybe Craig should have asked instead, "*Did* you touch it?")

Craig headed back to the orange caboose. Rick then headed to the red caboose. On his way over, Rick saw "someone sitting at the window." He entered, but saw nobody.

Meanwhile, back at the orange caboose, Karri felt like the "train had left the station." The movement was so realistic, that she "jumped out of her seat for a second" and then looked over to Craig in the red caboose. She, too, saw someone sitting at the window. Could it have been the lady that said "yes" to Craig's question?

A lady's scream was heard when they played back the recorder. It wasn't possible to determine if the scream emanated from the red, or the orange caboose.

Lastly, Craig, Rick and Karri headed to the dining car. Here were a few rooms, a bathroom and a dining area with table and chairs. There were nice glass shelves where one could have placed food or drink.

The trio sat at the table. Within moments things began to happen. Rick saw a gray mass, or shadow, run down the aisle. (A review of the audio picks up "It's us.")

Craig pulled out the ghost box and asked, "Can you give me a name?"

"Thomas Boyd," came the reply.

"We were just astonished," Craig recalled, as this was the first time that they had gotten "a clear first and last name" on an investigation.

A later check showed that the well-known explorer Thomas Boyd was in fact connected with the railroad industry in Australia. He was present at the grand opening of the Sidney to Hay railroad on July 4, 1882. Boyd had been instrumental in exploring that area with the Hovell and Hume exploration team back in 1824. He passed away in 1885 at the age of 88 years.

A voice on the ghost box said "Leave."

"I'm not leaving until you do something."

"Do it."

Craig's next comment was "I want some wine in the dining car."

A voice on the recorder as an EVP says "I am hungry."

The last couple of responses on the ghost box seemed to indicate that the speaker wanted conversation. Here was an intelligent voice, the same voice that gave his name as Thomas Boyd. What is he doing at the Railroad Museum in Green Bay, Wisconsin? Especially this time of year; it's much warmer in Australia!

The threesome took their turns at singing some country songs.

"I like those," Boyd comments on the songs.

Then footsteps came toward the table and again Craig felt a hand on his leg (under the table).

It was difficult to leave the car with all this activity going on, but others were waiting outside. On the way out Craig handed a voice recorder to Karri and asked if she would go into the Eisenhower by herself. Reluctantly, she agreed.

****

It was early in the morning and the team had an hour's drive back. So they packed up and headed home. They hope to "return when it is warmer to investigate the outside trains as well as talk to Thomas Boyd to learn more about him."

HER SPIRIT SPEAKS TO ME

By Craig Nehring

During the six years that I have been a paranormal investigator with my team, we have talked with ghosts that have passed on and heard their voices, but there was no personal involvement. That being said, we have made friends with some of the ghosts from the Berlin Tannery and in a few other places that we have investigated. We have even come to know them by name.

Justin Libigs, the owner of the First Ward School in Wisconsin Rapids, put it so clearly in my mind that ghosts are people too. They should be treated like people and not provoked like you see some teams do on television. I, for one, have never had a deeper understanding of the afterlife as I do now, yet I know very little. The last that thing I wanted to do was communicate with my girlfriend after she passed away. Rene used to joke with me that if she died from her illness, she would haunt me. It was a bad joke that I never wanted to think about.

I told her that she would live a long time and should stop worrying about it. Those words did not live up to the truth of the matter. What I am about to talk about sends people's minds reeling in many directions; that includes the views of my team as well. We can talk endlessly about religion and what we believe in, and that is for us all to take in and believe what we want to believe. For some people, the answer is that anyone we communicate with is a fallen angel (an angel of God that was kicked out of Heaven for various reasons, has fallen to earth and is now on the dark side.)

Yet, I have pastors coming to me to ask what I have found in my research, not because they want to judge me, but because they are curious as well. They enjoy hearing the voices that we have captured in so many places, including churches.

I want to touch on my background a little. I went to an all-Lutheran grade school. I was confirmed, baptized, and still go to church. Most of us have some type of belief system. Some may believe the spirits we talk to are evil, but I feel that is far from my truth. To dig deeper, I have considered that sixteen books are said to have been ripped out of the Bible (apocrypha) because they talk about communicating with loved ones after they pass as well as other subjects deemed unsuitable. It is an interesting read, and I personally believe that they are part of the original Bible.

Back to my understanding of life and death...I never thought that I would be talking to Rene, but find myself doing just that. I do not believe that she is a fallen angel of God, nor that she has turned to the dark side. I believe that she is here to guide and watch over her loved ones. Today I believe more strongly that death is not the end, but a new beginning.

A couple of weeks after she passed, I was asked by her family to drop off some of her things and try to communicate with Rene at her home in Rhinelander.

I used my ghost box version of the Franks Box from an electronics store. I prefer this model because I can get the real voice in real time as opposed to a computerized voice.

I began by asking if she wanted to talk. An answer came back, "Please talk."

A bit later her mom said, "Rene, I love you, and where are you?"

An answer came back, "Here, Mom."

I was so taken back from this, but yet sad. I missed her so much. I was talking with Rene but could not physically reach out and touch her and hold her. I wanted to confirm in my mind that this was indeed her, yet I knew in my heart that it really was.

I sent the voice recordings to Rene's niece who texted me, "Oh my gosh—that *is* Rene." She was happy to hear Rene's voice, yet sad. I seemed to have gained a greater piece of mind with her niece's confirmation—and her mom and dad's as well.

I continued to talk with Rene now and then, but wanted to have different questions answered. I did not ask how she died or if she knew that she was dead. I wanted to speak to her like she was alive. I asked questions that only she would know the answer to, like "What is your nickname."

A clear and certain voice returned, "Munchkin."

Rene has used that term a few times in our recent conversations. One day she started the conversation with "Munchkin here."

"What is the name of your little kitty that played with bottle caps?"

"Bella," was the return. I have no doubts: the voice and the answers are from Rene.

A male voice came though, "Craig, you need a new therapist." How ironic; I was seeing a grief counselor but realized that she was telling me the same things as I was hearing from my team members.

One day after work, I started talking to Rene about my day and how warm and nice the weather was.

"Yes it is," came the reply.

There are still questions in my mind like "Is there a warm and a cold where you are?" I know that she can see me as she has told me and others as well what I am wearing and the colors of my attire. My mind wanders again to "Where are you?" Some have told me she may be in a holding place until God returns to earth. Others say a parallel universe overlaps with ours a bit. Yet, we can't really know until we ourselves have died, so answers to that question are all conjecture.

At times, without being preempted with a question, Rene will say something like "Your dog is here."

I wonder, because I had two dogs pass away that I cared deeply about. I think to myself, "Do dogs go into the afterlife?" Some would say definitely not, but do we really know?

I recently read a book *The Three Heavens* written by John Hagee who writes of his life experiences. One chapter spoke of a little boy that drowned in a pool. He was clinically dead for quite some time but survived. The very cold water may have been what saved his life.

When asked by his mother what he remembered, the little boy replied, "Mom, I died and went to heaven."

Unsure of how to reply, his mom continued. "How do you know?"

"Because I saw a man who said his name was Jesus. Next to him was our dog sitting by his side. Then he went on and on about how heaven looked."

"How did you know that it was our dog?" Though the dog had died before her son was born, he knew the dog's name. So, do all dogs go to heaven?

I want to share with you a moment when I talked to Rene from my home in Berlin. I told Rene that I loved her and missed her very much. In return she said, "I love you too." The fact that I could talk to her from my home in Berlin as well as her home in Rhinelander brought tears to my eyes. I concluded that anyone who wanted to talk with her, or to loved ones of their own, would be heard no matter where they communicated from—and they might even get an answer.

The most poignant incident that I ever experienced since I have entered the world of the paranormal came two days after Valentine's Day 2016.

I woke up, crawled out of bed, and headed down the hallway to the bathroom. It was dark; I could not see what was about to happen to me. The entire area had turned ice cold, yet I felt something warm and soft. I stumbled backwards, catching myself before I fell. I knew in my heart that it was Rene. I grabbed the ghost box and asked, "Rene?"

"Here" came back. It was the clearest voice that I have ever heard from the ghost box. It could not be mistaken; it was truly Rene.

GHOST HUNTING EQUIPMENT

Swann Surveillance System

This system is similar to what one would use to record TV programs or for security on buildings. The DVR and four cameras can automatically record in total darkness and in all conditions at a distance up to 90 feet and for 30 continuous days. Typically, cameras are set up in separate rooms of an investigation site in areas where paranormal activities have been reported. Later, when a review of the combined footage is completed, any paranormal activities recorded can be transferred to a computer and posted to the FVGH website.

Stealth Camera

Like the trail cams that people use in the forest to view animals at night, this stealth camera can be set up almost anywhere. If something were to walk by it, the camera would either take video or pictures, record sound and provide pertinent information such as time, temperature—and even if there was a full moon that evening! The FVGH use the camera in many huge building investigations. It is often used outdoors during investigations at the Summerwind property near Land O' Lakes, Wisconsin.

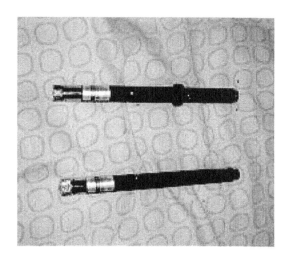

Laser Grid Lights

The laser grids cast many tiny green dots on a distant wall in the dark. A red-line grid casts lines on the wall in the distance. If something passes in front of the dots and the laser, an outline of a shadow would appear indicating a ghost had walked in front of it. The red-line grid would show the mass and contours of the spirit. Laser grids are used mostly in smaller rooms and hallways in haunted locations to attempt to capture spirit movement.

K2-Meter

This electro-magnetic field detector lights up when it comes in contact with positive or negative fields based on the intensity of the location of the ghost. Think of it as getting a fresh load of laundry out of the dryer and finding the clothes stick together, producing a static charge. This meter would recognize this and light up. This meter is difficult to use in detecting ghosts in buildings since it will also pick up electricity and outlets and powered objects close to them. All other power sources must be debunked before a conclusion can be made that something paranormal in nature is close by. The meter works best in open areas with no power. It comes in all shapes and sizes.

Ghost Box

This instrument is also known as a ghost box or Frank's Box. The latter was created by Frank Sumption. A newer model, the SB-7, is similar to Frank's Box and can be purchased on theghosthunterstore.com (an online site "run by real ghost hunters"). It is a device that scans white noise at milliseconds between radio stations to capture spirit communication in real time—like two people having a conversation. A ghost box runs both forward and backward in stations and on different frequencies that the ghosts use. Most paranormal groups use one of these three models.

Another type of recorder, the Ovilus, uses words from a dictionary, eliminating swear words. This differs from the above models in that the latter allows the ghost to say what it wants rather than using the dictionary vocabulary.

Rem Pod

Craig Nehring describes the Rem-Pod as "one of my favorite tools of the trade, very fun to use to detect something that may be following you down a hallway, a stairs, or into a room." The Rem-Pod is based along the lines of the K-2 meter, but in this case has four colorful lights on it and a small antenna that creates its own electromagnetic field around the body of the unit that can be easily influenced by materials and objects that conduct electricity. This allows for it to capture ghostly activity. If the ghost should touch the antenna or get close to the detector, the lights on top of the meter will indicate how close it is to the meter. The more lights, the closer the ghost is to the meter. A noise emits when the lights are on. This is a popular item seen in many ghost hunting programs.

Voice Recorder

The FVGH considers this recorder the most important tool for ghost-hunting. It is used on all investigations to help back up noises or voices that might have been heard by the participants. The recorder picks up voices that the human ear can't hear--electronic voice phenomenon (EVP), called "disembodied voices." The recorder can be used for 70 hours attached to cameras, hand held while walking around, or just left in one spot overnight. Files are then downloaded to the computer and later analyzed using a program called Audacity. This separates the voices from background noise and makes them easier to hear.

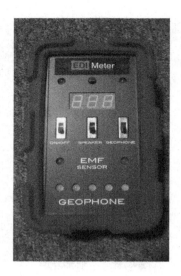

EDI Meter

This device utilizes a highly sensitive **electromagnetic field (EMF) sensor** programmed to detect fluctuations and strength of energy changes. Lights near the sensor indicate the amount of change. A speaker, that can be switched on or off, indicates a sharp change in EMF as well. The EDI also contains an **ambient temperature sensor** with a real-time digital display. Lights near the sensor illuminate to alert the user of temperature variations. A sharp drop might indicate a paranormal presence. The top red LEDs on the device would then blink rapidly. A very sensitive **geophone motion sensor**, with its built-in accelerometer, is programmed to pick up the slightest movement or vibration on the surface upon which the EDI is placed. A panel of lights will display a graph-like display based on the intensity of the movement. The EDI has a toggle switch to use when hand held.

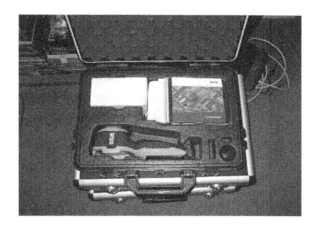

Thermal Camera

The Thermal Camera is the most sought after ghost-hunting tool made and very expensive (from $2,000 to $15,000). This device finds hot and cold spots on an infrared lens. The hot spots show up as red, and the cold spots as blue. It will also tell you the temperature of the spot you are looking for. Firefighters use these quite often to detect if there is heat from a fire they put out. Heating/cooling specialists can detect cold spots from air getting through walls in a house. Some ghost-hunting programs have caught full body apparitions in buildings. The FVGH use this camera down long hallways in large buildings. Craig Nehring relates, "We had one encounter with something we caught in an old church of a little girl, but I was unable to hit the record button in time."

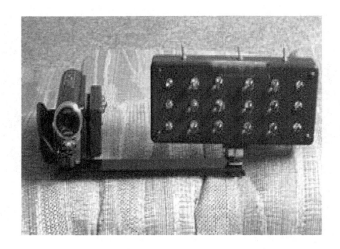

Full Spectrum Camcorder

This full-spectrum camcorder is similar to what people would use to shoot home videos, but in this camera there is a full-spectrum lens that shoots in all colors visible and invisible to the human eye. The camcorder can be set on a tripod or hand held while walking around. It can shoot still pictures as well as video and record for up to six hours.

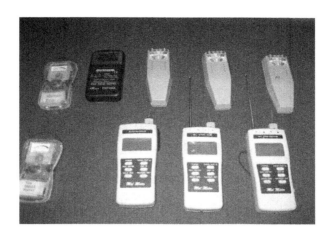

Mel Meter and K-2s

This stand-alone camera, an intelligent microprocessor-based instrument specifically designed for paranormal investigators, is much the same as the full spectrum camcorder. It is a hand-held meter; it also can be used as a stand-alone instrument that does not require a person's presence. There is a flip-stand on the back that can be angled for easy view from a table top. The Mel Meter measures EMF and temperature values quickly and easily.

We hope you enjoyed the forays into
the paranormal world with us. Visit
www.fvghosthunters.com, Join us
on an investigative tour...and,
tell your friends!

Made in the USA
Monee, IL
17 March 2020